HESTON BLUMENTHAL

IS THIS A COOKBOOK?

Adventures in the Kitchen

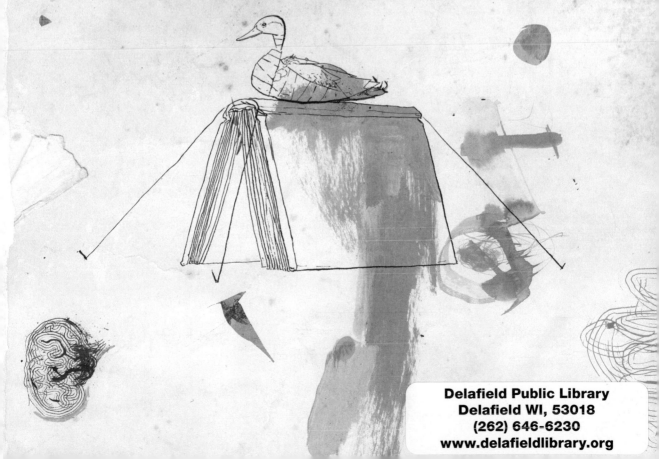

HESTON BLUMENTHAL

IS THIS A COOKBOOK?

Adventures in the Kitchen

ILLUSTRATION BY

Dave McKean

PHOTOGRAPHY BY

Haarala Hamilton

BLOOMSBURY PUBLISHING

LONDON · OXFORD · NEW YORK · NEW DELHI · SYDNEY

Contents

Dedicated to Sir Ken Robinson

'No man ever steps in the same river twice,
for it's not the same river and he's not the same man.'

HERACLITUS

'I think I can safely say that nobody understands
quantum mechanics…'

RICHARD FEYNMAN

'…*Yet!*'

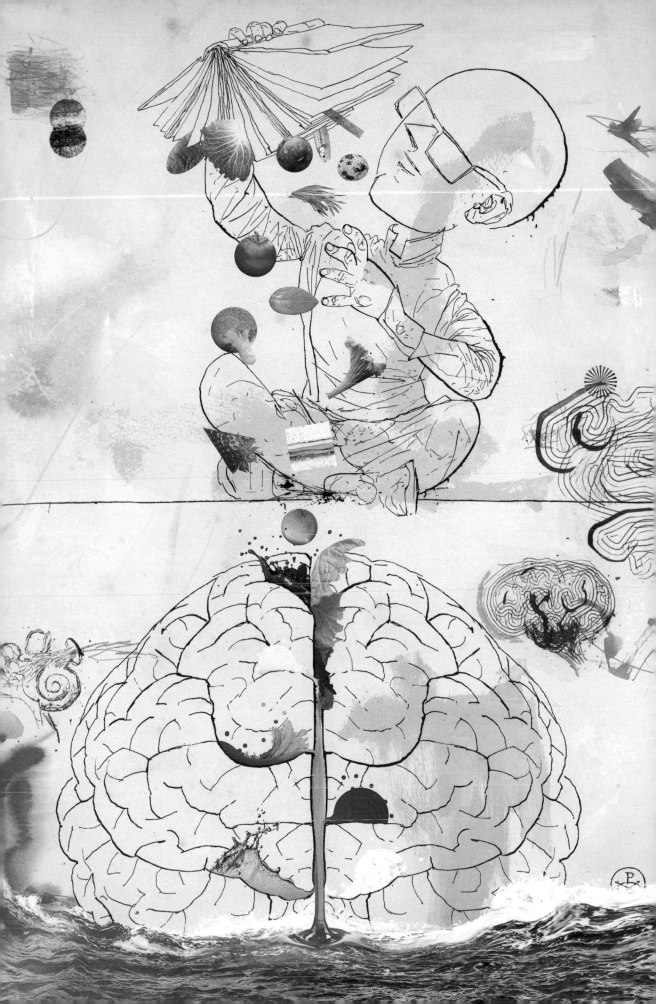

A quest for quantum gastronomy

Is this a cookbook? In answer to that question, you might reasonably reply, it's full of recipes so of course it's a cookbook. But perhaps there's more than one way of looking at this. Increasingly, I've come to see cooking in terms of quantum perspective – which, for me, at its most basic, means anything we do can be viewed in an infinite number of ways: how we experience it is determined by what perspective we choose. Is this book a collection of culinary instructions? An insight into how I think about food? An encouragement to think about your own relationship with food? A visual feast? Maybe it's all of these things and more. Maybe it's something else completely. It's up to you and your perspective.

How did I come to think of gastronomy in quantum terms? To explain that, I need to take you on a journey. I fell in love with food and cooking at 16 when I visited a restaurant in Provence called L'Oustau de Baumanière. Thirteen years later I opened my own bistro. I had no training and no ambitions for Michelin stars, but I guess I have a restless curiosity and a head full of questions and possibly a somewhat obsessive personality. I followed my nose (and tongue and tastebuds) and got caught up in a culinary world of precision and measurement and minuscule increments and timings and temperatures. Of endless testing and searching and refining. One of the catchphrases in my kitchen in the early days was 'Push on' and I pushed, pushed, pushed. Michelin stars followed. And other things besides – honorary degrees, a fellowship of the Royal Society of Chemistry, an OBE and the right to bear a coat of arms – but somehow it was never enough. Push on.

What was I chasing? Recognition? Affirmation? A sense of self-worth? I don't know. Yet. (I'm still a work-in-progress.) Increasingly, though, I became unsatisfied with the search for perfection. It seemed like a creative cul-de-sac – for me, at least – and I realised I needed to change my relationship with food and cooking. Was I a chef, with all the baggage that entails, or, when it came down to it, was I simply a human who cooks because cooking is my way of connecting with other people and sharing my beliefs? A lot of those beliefs remained largely unexplored. Perhaps it was time to do something about that.

One belief was sustainability – not just of the planet but also of ourselves, since food can be a great stimulus to the mind and emotions and our interconnectedness with others. Another was mindfulness – a word that's been overused and abused but, in essence, encourages us to be aware of our surroundings and the moment we're in and to take pleasure from it. Food and cooking offer opportunities to do just that. I've long emphasised the multi-sensory nature of cuisine, but I was mainly focused on how this sensory experience influences our perception of flavour. Now I wondered whether it might have a pivotal influence on our outlook and well-being as well.

Health and well-being had caught my attention in another way. Science has made us aware that our bodies contain a complex ecosystem of microbes that are known as the microbiome. And we're fast discovering that these hundred trillion organisms play a part in our digestion, our immune system and even our mind and our mood.

There's a microbiome-gut-brain axis that affects who we are and how we interact with the world. (As anyone whose nervousness before an exam has sent them to the toilet will already know.) And what we eat helps shape that ecosystem, so I became curious about what ingredients might have an effect on the microbiome.

These are among the ideas that have become important to me and, increasingly, have an influence on how I cook. Some of them, such as the role of water, are so complex they need a whole book devoted to them. (Riffle through the recipes that follow and you'll see – partly because I've highlighted it – just how essential water is, in a variety of forms, to almost any cooking you do.) But, where possible, you'll find them woven into the recipes that follow – whether it's getting to grips with microbe-friendly fermentation or serving up soups to suit different moods. However, more crucial to me than all of these is one overarching idea: the sustenance and celebration of the human imagination.

'We are educating people out of their creative capacities... our only hope for the future is to adopt a new conception of human ecology, one in which we start to reconstitute our conception of the richness of human capacity.' These words have been a constant inspiration to me. They come from a TED Talk entitled 'Do Schools Kill Creativity?' (www.ted.com/talks/sir_ken_robinson_do_schools_kill_creativity) given by Sir Ken Robinson, a brilliant educationalist who devoted his life to reforming the education system. It's still, as far as I know, the most-watched TED Talk of all time, which is not surprising because Ken presents his ideas with the clarity of a philosopher and the comic timing of a stand-up. I've watched it over and over and it still makes me laugh and makes me cry. His message is, in all senses, a universal one: our health, our well-being, our persistence on this planet depend on fostering the human imagination.

Ken was, of course, focused on teaching not cooking, so what has this got to do with food? The answer is in his follow-up TED Talk, 'Bring on the Learning Revolution!' (www.ted.com/talks/sir_ken_robinson_bring_on_the_learning_revolution) where he says we have built our education systems on a fast-food model, where standardisation is all. As a result, people opt out of education 'because it doesn't feed their spirit, it doesn't feed their energy or their passion'.

Feed the spirit. Food metaphors are so often invoked when we talk about human growth and well-being, perhaps because consuming food and water is the most essential activity for our existence. It's a fundamental part of who we are. Therefore, it seems to me, it offers a natural opportunity to encourage our creative capacities. We've got to do it on a daily basis anyway, so why not make cooking nourish our minds as well as our bodies? Maybe not every time – sometimes you've just got to get food on the table – but when we can.

How could this be conveyed in a cookbook? It couldn't – at least not in a conventional one, where the recipes are presented as a more-or-less inviolable set of instructions to be followed like a squaddie on a parade ground. I wanted to shift the perspective – to put a greater emphasis on a sense of fun and sensory stimulation and exploration and experimentation without any fear of failure. (As Ken Robinson reminds us: 'If you're not prepared to be wrong, you'll never come up with anything original.') And on freedom, where possible, from the tyranny of timings and the prison of precision. Forget the search for perfection, let's celebrate imperfection. If the dish doesn't look exactly like the photo but it tastes pretty good and you've enjoyed cooking it, then that's surely a success.

And this is where quantum gastronomy comes in. I know what you're thinking – we're back to Boffin Blumenthal and a lot of complicated science. But bear with me: we'll be out of the lab and back in the kitchen in a jiffy.

A century or so ago, scientists developed a branch of physics called quantum mechanics, in which they explored the behaviour of infinitesimally tiny particles of matter (quanta). They discovered these subatomic things could be in more than one place at once, or spin in different directions at the same time. In the most famous thought experiment designed to illustrate the perplexing complexity of quantum mechanics, Schrödinger's cat is both alive and dead in a sealed box. All seemingly illogical, impossible things that most of us find difficult to reconcile with our experience of the physical world.

What strikes me, though, is that in our emotional, imaginative worlds we encounter contradictory quantum dualities all the time and take them in our stride. Our body is at a desk, say, but our mind is in Acapulco. We can harbour anger and sadness at the same time. Are the tears on a face in a photograph tears of happiness or sadness? Without more information, we accept both possibilities exist. This duality is part of how we experience the world: we're constantly choosing between different perspectives.

Something similar, it seems to me, happens when we go in the kitchen. Every cooking session inevitably involves a lot of assessing and measuring and timing and monitoring and cold calculations. At the same time, it offers sensory and physical pleasures (the aroma of roasting tomatoes; the satisfaction of chopping and slicing), and triggers memories and associations and emotions that add another dimension to the experience. Both have their place in cooking, but often the mindful aspects end up stifled by our desire to follow the recipe exactly and not make a mistake.

This book, then, is structured to accommodate this quantum split that happens in the kitchen. A split I think of as human being and human doing. Human doing is the culinary task with all its strictures and structures. Human being, on the other hand, is all that stuff that makes us, er, human beings. Our ability to respond to cooking in an imaginative way – noticing things, finding connections, responding emotionally, taking everything in and turning it into experiences, consciousness and our own personalised version of reality.

So, in general, on the left-hand page of each recipe spread is the human doing: the list of ingredients and amounts, with a set of instructions. On the right-hand page you'll find the human being, which is in a sense me heckling the recipe, drawing attention to whatever emotions, thoughts, suggestions the act of cooking prompts in me. The things that, for me, make a recipe exciting – a sort of portal to the imagination and culinary creativity. How you engage with these quantum possibilities is of course up to you. And probably depends on your perspective and how you feel at any particular moment. Sometimes, maybe all you want to do is get it done. Or maybe, the first time you make something, you just want to concentrate on getting it right.

Other days maybe you find yourself taking a more relaxed, languorous approach. It will be interesting to discover if you prefer one way or the other.

I should also let you know about another split. You'll encounter a second Heston among these pages. He wasn't invited and I'm not sure how to explain exactly what Little Heston is – a symbol perhaps of the

inner child or

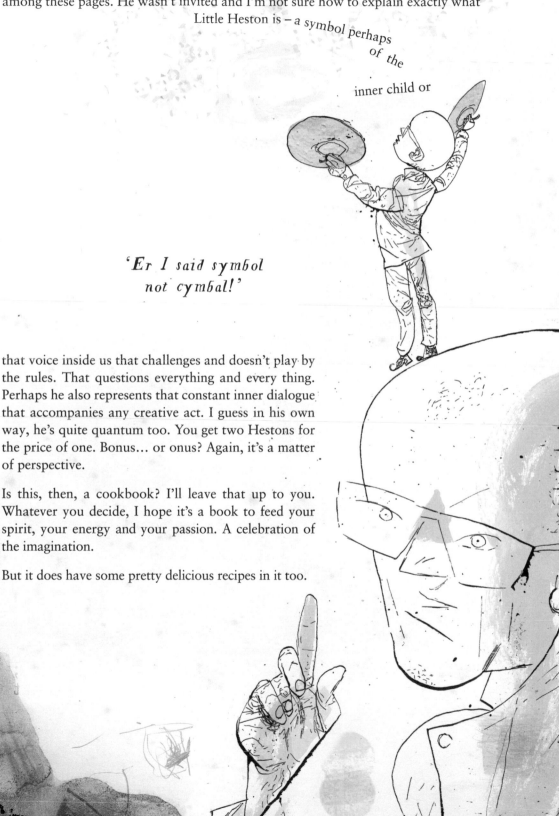

'*Er I said symbol not cymbal!*'

that voice inside us that challenges and doesn't play by the rules. That questions everything and every thing. Perhaps he also represents that constant inner dialogue that accompanies any creative act. I guess in his own way, he's quite quantum too. You get two Hestons for the price of one. Bonus… or onus? Again, it's a matter of perspective.

Is this, then, a cookbook? I'll leave that up to you. Whatever you decide, I hope it's a book to feed your spirit, your energy and your passion. A celebration of the imagination.

But it does have some pretty delicious recipes in it too.

Human Doing

HUMAN BEING

1

The Mindful Sandwich

*Why don't we take a moment
and slow things down?*

A Mindful Sandwich

•

Bacon Butty

•

Jubilee Coronation Chicken

•

Kimcheese Toastie

•

Pea and Ham Soup-in-a-Sandwich

•

Prawn Cocktail Salad Sandwich

•

Egg and Rocket

•

Pan Bagnat

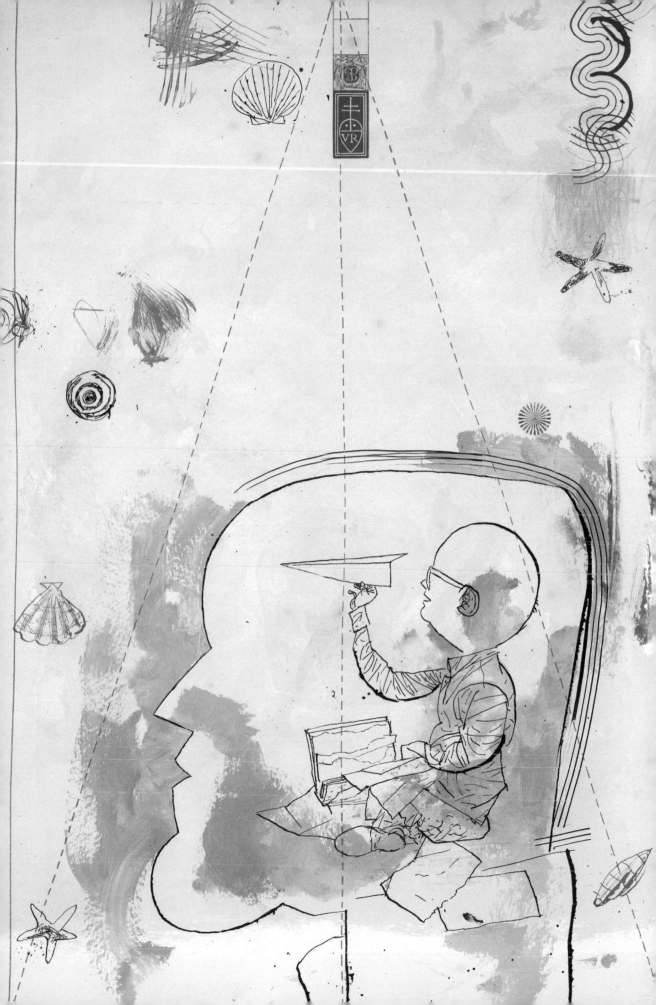

A MINDFUL SANDWICH

A while back I took a plane journey during which I was served
an airline meal. Most of you'll know the drill – tray with an
array of little plastic containers housing something savoury,
something sweet, plastic cutlery, sachets of salt and pepper.
Not something we normally take much pleasure in.
But this time, I figured I'd shift my perspective.
Took my time over each part of the meal, chewed thoughtfully,
identifying flavours and aromas, enjoying the textures.
It was surprisingly satisfying and utterly absorbing –
so much so that I still hadn't finished when the stewardess
came to take the tray away.

Food can be many things: fuel, of course, which we need
to exist, but also a way to live in the present moment,
by focusing on what's presented to the senses.

It's no accident that many well-being techniques,
from Eastern philosophy to yoga to meditation, encourage
us to 'live in the moment', suggesting it makes us
appreciate more what's around us,
helps disburden ourselves of distractions,
and enriches our life by simplifying it.
This can have a positive effect on our
mental health and our happiness.

Whether this is true or not,
we have to find out for ourselves.
But maybe one way to explore the idea is through food.

More recently, I had another 'moment' that was even more extraordinary, and much more emotional. For the photoshoot for the pics you see on the previous spread I chose to go to *Hyde Park* because it's just round the corner from my restaurant *Dinner By Heston Blumenthal.* It was only, though, when we got there that I remembered what a strong connection I had to the place, and it hit me like a brick.

When I was about seven we lived in a grotty basement flat in a posh block nearby. The park was my playground and I was there almost every day. Memories flooded back, unstoppably – playing football with jumpers for goalposts, learning to ride a bike, breaking into the police station! (and the boathouse!), being fished out of the fountain at *Marble Arch,* eating the sand in *Rotten Row* to see what it tasted like, diving into the *Serpentine* and coming up covered in leaves.

I had no idea, of course, that one day I'd be a three-star chef and open a restaurant overlooking the park. The contrast, and the sense of time passing, was almost overwhelming.

I hadn't been in the park for years and thoughts and feelings and nostalgia welled up uncontrollably and had me in tears. I ended up lost in a moment, down a rabbit hole of my own memories and imagination, living a dream – and all because I was looking for a place to eat a sandwich. Food can have this kind of power, if we let it.

Of course, if you want to try this out, you don't have to take a plane ride, or even visit *Hyde Park.* How about the next time you buy a sandwich to eat at your desk, or raid the fridge at lunchtime, you choose to make it a *Mindful Sandwich* and see what happens?

Me, I'm going to make a cheese sandwich, but you can make or buy whatever you want: something simple and familiar and nostalgic, or something new and adventurous, or whatever.

What we're exploring here is not what we eat but how we eat it.

I decided on one of the simplest, commonest and most popular sandwiches, because I'm curious as to how this idea will work in its most pared-back state. So, I've got butter smeared on a slice from a packet of white bread, topped with thin slabs of Cheddar and another slice of bread.

You might choose different cheese or bread or add slices of cucumber, or all sorts. Feel free to do whatever you feel like. After all, it's your sandwich and your emotions. For me, just the smell and the feel of the bread takes me back to childhood.

'Did you know that, until recently, in France it was against the law to eat at your desk? It's Article R.4428-19 of the Code du Travail.'

'Bon appètit'

Continued on next page...

21

After buying or making your sandwich, but before you eat it, perhaps it's worth thinking about where you want to eat it. I believe place and context can have a huge influence on how we experience our food and thus even on how we perceive flavour.

So, give your sandwich a chance.
If you've been working all morning,
you've earned yourself some time.
Maybe hunt out a park bench. Register the
sounds surrounding you, from the throb of car
engines in the distance to the tweets of birds.

Close your eyes if you want – it can help
concentrate the mind and the senses.
Feel the packet under your fingers.
Hear the sound as the packaging rips.
How does the bread feel between your fingers?
What about the contrast of the crust?
How does the bread smell as you bring
it towards your mouth? Is there
a wheatiness? A yeastiness?
(Maybe even a sourness if you've gone posh
with your sarnie.)

What do you feel as the bread gently touches the
top lip? A softness? Does it feel the same on
the bottom lip? And what sensations do you get
on your upper gum, your lower gum, as you
press down? Are there differences?

It's often said Buddhist monks chew each mouthful
at least thirty times, and it's interesting exploring
what a more extended chew brings to the experience.
But don't get hung up on counting.
We're focusing on flavours not figures.

22

*Indeed, what tastes and flavours do you find?
Can you detect every ingredient?
Do they work together?
Do some flavours come through later than others?
What's happening with the saliva, and what about
the sweetness? Are the sugars changing?*

*What about the variety of textures and what they
bring to the experience?*

*Do some flavours linger longer? And what associations
do they trigger? Does it transport you somewhere else –
other places? Other memories?*

For me, food has that magic: if we let it –
if we let the stimulation flow and register it as
it happens – it can slow down the frenetic pace
of life, focus our senses and confer a sense of
well-being, of being fulfilled rather than feeling
full. (I find that when I eat like this – with
gut feeling and curiosity – I eat less and feel
healthier for it. But maybe that's just me.)
You can get in touch with yourself and let
stress, worries and distracting or disturbing
thoughts fade into the background. It's not
something I do all the time, just whenever
I choose to consume food in a mindful way.

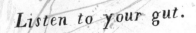

Listen to your gut.

BACON BUTTY
What do you want from a bacon sarnie?

There's the seductive sizzle when it's cooking.
There's that irresistible aroma that draws you in like a magnet.
Then there are those delicious contrasts – smoked and unsmoked,
crisp and soft, savoury and a touch of sweetness.

I've taken inspiration from Mrs Beeton for an extra textural
contrast. Included in her *Cookery and Household Management*
is a recipe for *Toast Sandwiches*, in which a piece of toast
is the filling between two slices of buttered bread.
She claims it 'will be found very tempting to the appetite
of an invalid'. I don't know about that but having both bread
and toast adds another layer of crispness and softness that will
hopefully be found tempting to everyone, invalid or not.

Bacon Butty

MAKES 2

4 rashers unsmoked back bacon
6 rashers smoked streaky bacon
2 tbsp oil
20g salted butter
4 slices of white bread

For the sauce

2 tbsp French's mustard
2 tbsp tomato ketchup
2 tbsp mayonnaise

Place the bacon rashers between two sheets of baking paper. Use a rolling pin to roll the bacon until very thin, then discard the paper and slice each rasher in half.

Heat the oil in a large frying pan, add all the bacon rashers and fry, turning frequently, until cooked through and crispy. Remove the back bacon rashers and set aside, allowing the remaining streaky rashers to fry a little longer until crisp and caramelised.

In the meantime, for the sauce, mix the mustard, ketchup and mayonnaise together in a small bowl.

Butter two of the slices of bread and set aside.

To assemble, toast the other two slices of bread, butter them and top with the bacon. Sandwich together with the slices of untoasted, buttered bread (so you have two sandwiches, each with one side bread and one side toast).

Serve immediately, with the sauce on the side to use as a dip between each bite.

Of course, you can skip this
step and you'll still have a great butty.
Rolling it, though, tenderises the bacon and ensures
it doesn't pucker and frill up so much during
cooking. Because it's flatter, there's more surface
area in contact with the pan, so it goes nice
and crispy.

Dead simple to make, this is similar to
a burger sauce but with the mustard
element upped. For me, French's - the classic
hot-dog mustard - is the one for the job
because it has a bigger punch of acidity than
most other brands and is more piccalilli-like.

Quick! Get that butter on there while it's hot.
I love it when the heat of the toast melts the butter.

JUBILEE
CORONATION CHICKEN

Fancy a sandwich with a bit of history?

Created in 1953 for the queen's Coronation Luncheon (when it was served as *Poulet Reine Elizabeth*), Coronation chicken was still a firm favourite in the 1970s, when I was growing up. Me and my mum loved it, and it was a key part of any picnic we had in Windsor Great Park or Virginia Water. Like a lot of 70s classics it has fallen out of favour, but it can be absolutely delicious. So why not give retro a go?

Jubilee Coronation Chicken

MAKES 2

200g cooked boneless chicken breast or legs
20g dried apricots
70g mayonnaise
15g mango chutney
2 tsp medium curry powder
¼ tsp Worcestershire sauce
Salt and black pepper
4 slices of white or wholegrain bread
Salted butter, as needed

For the dry 'dip'

2 tbsp desiccated coconut
2 tbsp flaked almonds

Dice the chicken. Chop the dried apricots into small pieces and combine with the chicken.

In a separate bowl, mix the mayonnaise, mango chutney, curry powder and Worcestershire sauce together well and season with salt and freshly ground black pepper. Add this mixture to the chicken and stir to combine. Cover and set aside in the fridge until you are ready to assemble your sandwiches.

To make the 'dry dip', toast the desiccated coconut in a dry, small non-stick pan until golden. Tip into a bowl and set aside. Add the flaked almonds to the pan and toast in the same way. Tip the toasted almonds onto a board and roughly chop them, then mix with the coconut.

Butter all 4 slices of bread and create two sandwiches, using a generous amount of the chicken filling in each. Slice as you please – just be sure to dip the sandwiches into the bowl of 'dry dip' between each bite.

Any cooked chicken can be used: leftovers from your own roast chicken or store-bought are both suitable.

For the bread, you can of course play around with baguettes or sourdough. But for me, this is another sandwich where only soft bread will do because it brings a textural contrast I really like.

The fruity element in the original was an apricot purée, but you often find modern recipes using raisins or sultanas instead. I'm not generally a fan of raisins in meat dishes, but here it works, so feel free to sneak in raisins in place of the apricots if you want.

If you're making this ahead of time, you might find that the chicken greedily sucks up a lot of the mayo mixture. If this happens, just add a tablespoonful or so of water, which will loosen it.

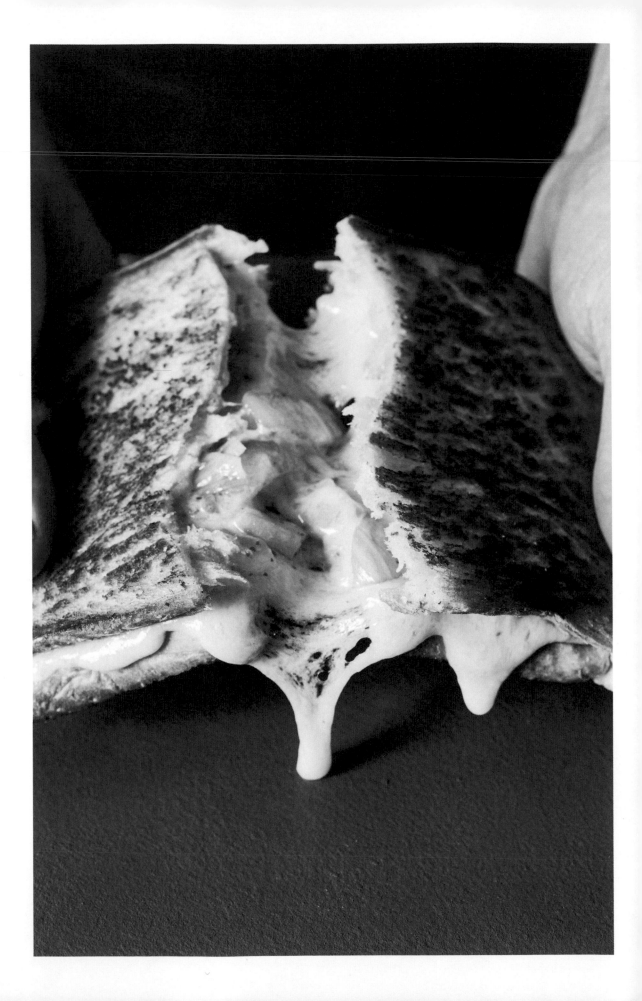

KIMCHEESE TOASTIE
Korean Rarebit, anyone?

I'm very interested in the two-way relationship between our gut and our brain, so naturally I'm excited about ingredients that seem to have a beneficial effect on our gut – and potentially therefore on our brains too. Fermented foods like kimchi are often put forward as particularly gut-friendly. Is this in fact the case? The best way to find out, it seems to me, is to try them out yourself and listen to your gut. Mine seems to like them so I've developed a variety of flavourful dishes featuring fermentation that you'll find in Chapter 8.

Here, though, that spicy, sharp, crunchy cabbage finds a place in a sandwich inspired by the melted-cheese classic Welsh Rarebit and the Breville-browned toasties of my youth.

Whether it's good for your gut or not, it's a great snack. There's a moment eating it when you just find that your shoulders relax. You'll see.

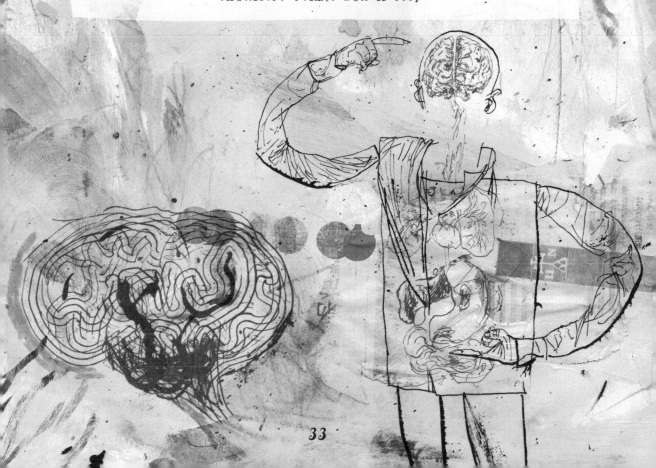

Kimcheese Toastie

SERVES 1

1 wedge Kimchi (page 277), finely chopped
2 slices of white bread
120g Cheddar, thinly sliced
Black pepper
About 50g salted butter

Spread the chopped kimchi on a slice of bread and lay the cheese slices on top.
Season with freshly ground black pepper. Sandwich together with the second slice
of bread and butter the top generously.

Heat a frying pan over a medium-low heat. Add the sandwich, buttered side
down, and toast until golden underneath, buttering the top side once the sandwich
is in the pan. Toast the sandwich slowly, turning it regularly
and adding more butter if needed.

Once the cheese begins to ooze out and the bread is golden and crispy, remove the
sandwich from the pan, slice and eat straight away.

Have a smell and a little nibble of that kimchi
before you add it. What do you smell and taste –
a tangy sharpness? Just think how
that's going to both bring flavour contrast
and cut the richness of that cheese.

Rich dishes often benefit from pops
of something sharp and acidic. It's something
to think about when you're cooking cheesy
dishes – kimchi could add something to a
mac 'n' cheese or a cabbage gratin – but
equally it could bring balance to, say, an
oily fish. Then there's that crunch, which
will add a textural contrast as well.

That medium–low heat is key if you want
a crisply crunchily browned outside and
a smoothly oozy filling. Have the heat
too high and the exterior might be overdone
by the time the interior has reached
your desired level of melt. It's worth
keeping an eye on it – and maybe
a prodding finger, too.

PEA AND HAM
SOUP-IN-A-SANDWICH

What is fresh?

There's a lot of snobbery surrounding fresh peas vs frozen. My question would be: which is fresher – a pod that's perhaps taken several days to reach the market place, or a pea that's been frozen almost as soon as it's been picked?

Here petits pois are the star of the show, not just because of their flavour. Those plump green spheres are a perfect example of what I call 'flavour encapsulation' – bursting beneath the teeth to give little spurts of sweetness. A contrast that adds interest to the sandwich and textural pleasure.

Pea and Ham Soup-in-a-Sandwich

MAKES 2

170g frozen petits pois, defrosted
50g crème fraîche
10–12 fresh mint leaves
Salt and black pepper
4 slices of wholegrain bread
Salted butter, as needed
65g pulled or shredded smoked ham hock

Put the peas into a bowl and stir through the crème fraîche to bind them. Finely chop the mint and stir into the mixture. Season generously with salt and freshly ground black pepper.

To assemble, butter the slices of bread. Spread 2 bread slices with the pea mixture and top with the shredded ham hock. Sandwich together with the other buttered bread slices.

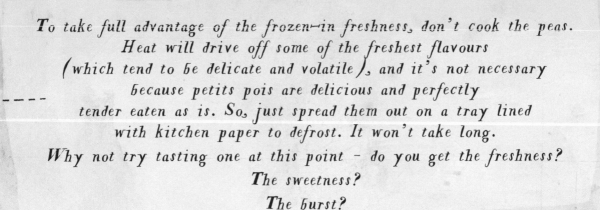

To take full advantage of the frozen-in freshness, don't cook the peas.
Heat will drive off some of the freshest flavours
(which tend to be delicate and volatile), and it's not necessary
because petits pois are delicious and perfectly
tender eaten as is. So, just spread them out on a tray lined
with kitchen paper to defrost. It won't take long.
Why not try tasting one at this point – do you get the freshness?
The sweetness?
The burst?

If you want to add a bit of zip to the mix,
stir a tablespoonful of wholegrain mustard
into the crème fraîche.

You can lightly season the ham
if you feel it needs it. And you
can also use a good smoked ham in
this sandwich, if you've not got
shredded ham hock.

PRAWN COCKTAIL SALAD SANDWICH

What's your secret food fave?

Have I mentioned already how much I love sandwiches?

So, if I can find a way to put one of my favourite dishes between two slices of bread, I'll do it.

Many of you will already know how much I like prawn cocktail. In the past I might have called it a guilty pleasure but, increasingly, I find that notion nonsensical, particularly when it comes to food.

Dr Gabor Maté talks about how much 'unaware' stress affects our lives and our health. Feelings such as guilt can exert just this kind of stress, and act as a dampener on human connectivity. As far as I'm concerned, if you appreciate and love what you consume, it'll have a positive effect on you.

Prawn Cocktail Salad Sandwich

MAKES 2

For the Marie Rose sauce

20g mayonnaise

25g tomato ketchup

½ vanilla pod, seeds scraped (or ¼ tsp vanilla bean paste)

Few drops of Worcestershire sauce

Squeeze of lemon juice, to taste

Salt and black pepper

For the sandwich

70g peeled, cooked king prawns

40g Iceberg lettuce, thinly sliced

4 cherry tomatoes, quartered

½ avocado, finely diced

4 slices of wholegrain bread

Salted butter, as needed

To make the sauce, combine all the ingredients in a bowl and mix well, seasoning with salt and freshly ground black pepper to taste.

Add the cooked prawns to the sauce and toss well to coat evenly.

Combine the dressed prawns, lettuce, cherry tomatoes and diced avocado in a bowl.

To assemble, butter the slices of bread and sandwich together with the prawn cocktail salad, being generous with the filling.

Eat soon after assembling to enjoy these sandwiches at their best.

You can, of course, use whatever bread you want but I like something with a bit of give, a bit of softness. For me, it's one of the textural pleasures of the dish. That and the crunch of a crisp Iceberg lettuce.

Unless it's 30°C outside, you won't find the butter in the Blumenthal fridge. I don't like it when it's too hard to spread and starts tearing the bread as you smear it on.

Go easy on the lemon juice, adding a little at a time, so that you get the level of acidity and the thick or thin consistency you prefer.

You could make a double quantity of Marie Rose sauce, put half in the salad and have the rest on the side, to dip your sandwich into between bites.

EGG AND ROCKET
How about livening up a classic?

Traditionally, this'd be egg and garden cress. But cress put me in mind of watercress, whose sharpness I figured might enliven the sandwich, giving it a bit of a kick.

It worked well, so I upped the ante to rocket's punchy pepperiness. You could try it at some point with each of these three leaves to see whether you prefer one or the other.

Or maybe a mix could be the way to go?

Egg and Rocket

3 large eggs
40g mayonnaise
2 tsp English mustard
Few drops of sherry vinegar
Salt and black pepper
15g pickled gherkins (e.g. Mrs Elswood), very finely chopped
4 slices of wholegrain bread
Salted butter, as needed
2 handfuls of wild rocket

Place the eggs in a small pan. Pour on enough **water** to cover and put the lid on. Bring to the boil over a high heat. Once the **water** is boiling, take the pan off the heat and set a timer for 8 minutes. Remove the eggs from the **water** and leave to cool, then peel the eggs and separate the whites from the yolks.

In a small bowl, mash the egg yolks together with 15g of the mayonnaise and the 2 tsp mustard. Add a little sherry vinegar to taste and season the mixture with a little salt and freshly ground black pepper.

Finely chop the egg whites and place in a bowl with the pickled gherkins. Add the remaining 25g mayonnaise to this mixture and season generously with salt and freshly ground black pepper.

To assemble, butter the slices of bread. To layer up the sandwiches, spread the yolk mixture on two of the slices, cover with the egg-white mix then top with a handful of rocket leaves. Lay the other bread slices on top and press lightly.

We tend to think of an egg as a single unit,
but in fact the yolk and the white are two very different things
– different colours, different textures, different flavours.
By separating the two out, you can take advantage
of those differences and bring variety to the sandwich.

I really love the combination of egg
and mayo, which is deeply nostalgic for
me, probably from the tin-foil-wrapped
sandwiches eaten on Cornish beaches when
I was on holiday as a kid. I've got a bit
of a thing for Devilled Eggs as well.

The sharp acidity of the pickled gherkins
balances the richness of the boiled eggs
and mayo perfectly.

PAN BAGNAT
When does I + I = 3?

Actually, in cooking, I'd say that equation often holds good: you put together a promising set of ingredients, but the end result far exceeds expectations. You might look at this recipe and think that it's basically a niçoise salad sandwich but wait till you try it – something magical happens during the process of wrapping up the sandwich and compressing it for a while, letting the juices from the vinaigrette and the tomatoes slowly soak into the bread. Neither a salad nor a sandwich but something wonderfully other.

For me, there's a strong nostalgia in this dish, too. Memories of teenage holidays by the sea in the Camargue. There'd be a man walking the shore with a basket of pan bagnats. I'd buy one and bite in and get those powerful punches of saltiness, pickledness and acidity from the olives, the anchovies and, above all, the capers. In the end, as far as I'm concerned, this sandwich is all about the capers and that stint steeping in the fridge.
(Pan bagnat means 'bathed bread'.)

Nowadays, it's very difficult to find pan bagnat in France, so you'll probably have to make a trip to Nice's Vieille Ville. Or have a go at this recipe and enjoy the Mediterranean smells and flavours, and the sensory and physical pleasures of prepping a simple dish.

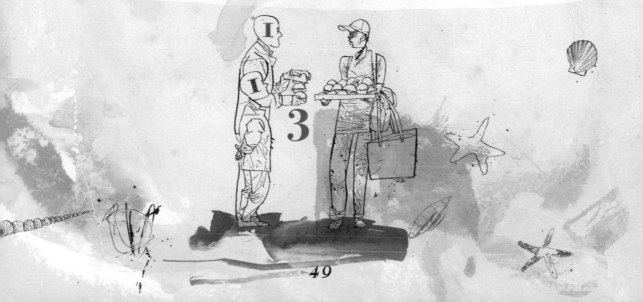

49

Pan Bagnat

MAKES 1

20g finely sliced onion
100g French beans, stalk ends trimmed
2 large eggs
2 tsp Dijon mustard
4 tsp tarragon vinegar (or white wine vinegar)
3 tbsp olive oil, plus extra if needed
185g tin tuna in brine, drained (140g drained weight)
40g best-quality pitted black olives, sliced
1 tbsp capers, drained
2 vine tomatoes, trimmed and sliced
6 Little Gem lettuce leaves (inner leaves are best)
Salt flakes and black pepper
1 medium boule (plump, round loaf)
8 fresh basil leaves
4 anchovy fillets, rinsed and drained

Place the sliced onion in a small bowl of cold **water** and leave to soak for
5–10 minutes to soften the flavour.

Bring a small pan of salted **water** to the boil. Add the green beans,
bring back to the boil and cook until *al dente*
(tender enough to eat but still with a bit of bite). Immediately drain and plunge
the beans into a bowl of iced **water**. Once cooled, drain and set aside.

Place the eggs in a small pan. Pour on enough **water** to cover and put the lid on.
Bring to the boil over a high heat. The moment you see it boiling, take the pan
off the heat and set a timer for 8 minutes. Once the time is up, drain the eggs,
then peel and slice.

Mix the mustard and tarragon vinegar together in a small bowl and whisk in the
olive oil until the mixture emulsifies. Drain the onion and stir into the dressing.

Put the drained tuna, olives, capers, tomatoes and lettuce into a large bowl.
Drizzle the dressing over the tuna mix. Add the green beans and toss gently to coat
all the elements evenly in the dressing. Season with salt and freshly ground black
pepper to taste.

Slice the top off the boule and set aside. Lay the sliced hard-boiled egg in the loaf
(or large bun or bap if using). Roughly tear the basil leaves and scatter these and
the anchovies over the egg slices. Pile in the tuna salad and cover with the top of
the loaf, tucking in all the salad around the edges.

Wrap the loaf tightly in a clean tea towel and set aside in the fridge for several
hours (or even better, overnight) for the flavours to steep.

For the modern pan bagnat, French bakers started making a round loaf about 20cm in diameter specifically for this purpose. But you can use any round loaf or large bun or bap.

This should take about 5 minutes, but trust your mouth rather than your watch - taste one to see after 3 minutes and judge from there.

These beans bring a bit of firmer texture to the salad, which is why you want them al dente. But beans will carry on cooking after they've been removed from the pan. Plunging them in a bowl of iced water stops this.

Do you think food tastes different depending on the context - where? when? with whom? - in which you eat it? Would you experience this sandwich differently at your desk compared to, say, by the coast in summer?

2

Heston's Breakfast Bar

When do you want to start the day?

Banana and Parsley Smoothie

•

Parsnip Granola

•

Tomato and Coffee Muffins

•

Eggs: from Scrambled to Soufflé Omelette

•

Green Eggs and Ham

•

Bacon and Egg Porridge

Heston's Breakfast Bar

When do you want to start the day?

Banana and Parsley Smoothie

•

Parsnip Granola

•

Tomato and Coffee Muffins

•

Eggs: from Scrambled to Soufflé Omelette

2

BANANA AND PARSLEY SMOOTHIE

What do you think of this flavour combo? What do you think it might taste like?

Perhaps you find it an unlikely combination.
For me, one of the pleasures of cooking is taking that
step into the unknown and discovering something
unexpectedly wonderful.

A greenish, unripe banana is more starchy than
sweet and has an affinity with parsley, the two of
them combining to produce something that's somehow
neither banana nor parsley, neither sweet nor
savoury. A unique and utterly delicious flavour.

Banana and Parsley Smoothie

MAKES 1 LARGE SMOOTHIE

1 peeled partially ripe banana (about 100g)
10g roughly picked fresh parsley
150g kefir milk
50g cucumber, roughly chopped
1 tsp inulin prebiotic powder (optional)

Place all the ingredients in a jug blender and blitz until smooth,
stopping to scrape down the sides a few times.

You'll really get the full effect of this flavour combination if you use a partially ripe banana: one that is light green in colour and only just starting to turn yellow.

Press the button to blitz – 'until smooth', I've advised, but it's not the smoothness that hits you once it's done.

First it's the colour – a hugely appealing pale green that suggests a delightful, delicate freshness. Then as you lift the lid you get a wonderful burst of aroma with hints of, what, almond? Marzipan? Tap the glass and you can sense just how light and airy the texture is.

And what about the flavour? What's in that first sip? Can you taste cucumber? Parsley? A lactic tang from the kefir?...

Continued on next page...

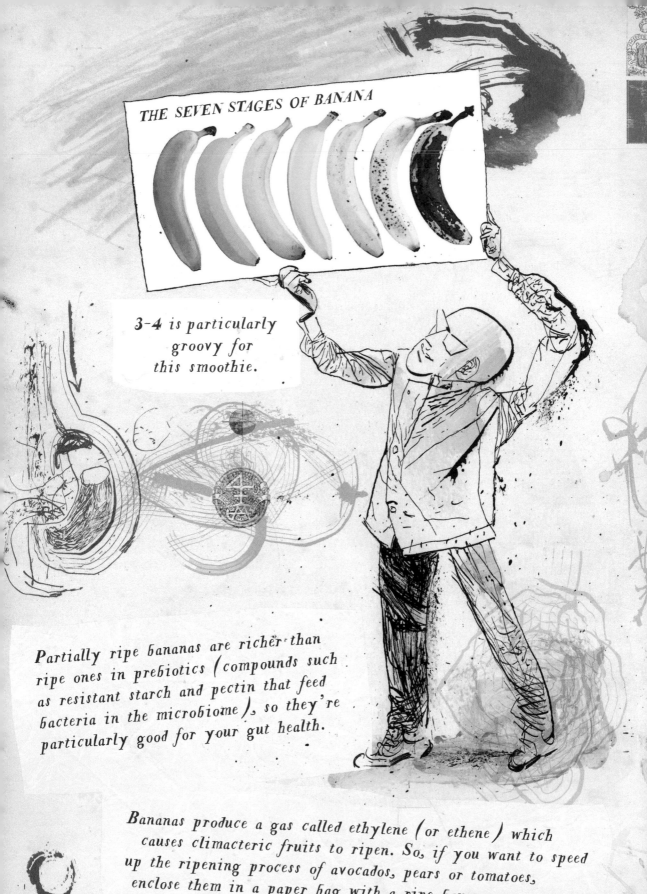

THE SEVEN STAGES OF BANANA

3-4 is particularly groovy for this smoothie.

Partially ripe bananas are richer than ripe ones in prebiotics (compounds such as resistant starch and pectin that feed bacteria in the microbiome), so they're particularly good for your gut health.

Bananas produce a gas called ethylene (or ethene) which causes climacteric fruits to ripen. So, if you want to speed up the ripening process of avocados, pears or tomatoes, enclose them in a paper bag with a ripe banana.

'Tell them the
farting story,
Heston'

'I'm not
sure the readers
want to hear
about that...'

'OK, I'll tell it.
This inulin is
a form of fibre.

It's good for your gut health but
your body needs to get used to it, so
it's good to start small and work your
way up. During recipe development, he
once added a couple of tablespoons by
mistake and, for the next twelve hours,
he really put the art into farting.
Talk about an edible
whoopee cushion!!'

'Moving on...
I wonder what this would
be like as an ice cream.
How about putting a batch
into the churner
to find out?'

59

PARSNIP GRANOLA
Parsnips... for breakfast!?

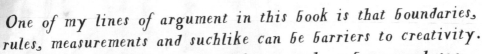

One of my lines of argument in this book is that boundaries, rules, measurements and suchlike can be barriers to creativity. Some of my most famous dishes – such as bacon-and-egg ice cream – have come from exploring familiar ingredients in an unfamiliar or unexpected context. From putting them somewhere they're not 'supposed' to be. Sometimes questioning everything means disregarding received opinion and following your mouth and nose and flavour memories instead.

So why not parsnip for breakfast? It'll grate to the right sort of texture. It has a touch of sweetness that'll suit the other ingredients. And – as we all know from winter feasts or Christmas – it roasts to a delicious nuttiness in the oven.

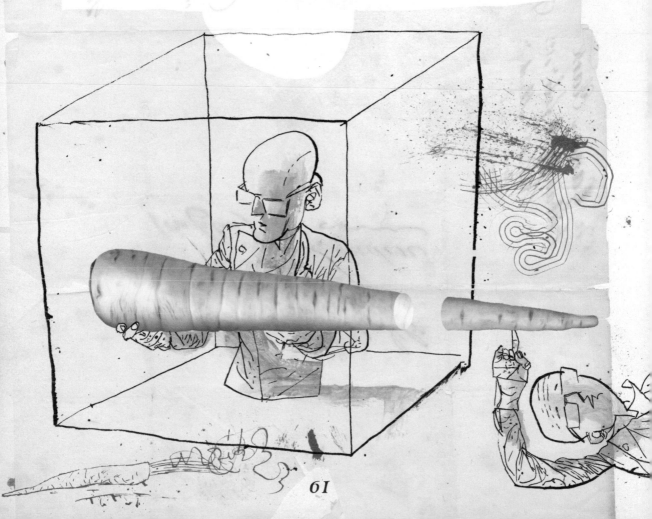

Parsnip Granola

100g honey or maple syrup
1 tsp salt
Pinch of ground cinnamon
75g grated peeled parsnip
120g oats
50g chopped hazelnuts
Oat or hemp milk, to serve (optional)

Preheat the oven to 180°C/Fan160°C/Gas 4 and line a large tray with baking paper.

Put the honey, salt and cinnamon into a small pan and bring to a simmer over a moderate heat. Stir in the grated parsnip and cook for 2 minutes.

Combine the oats and hazelnuts in a bowl and pour in the honey parsnip mix. Stir well to combine, then spread out on the tray. Bake for 18–25 minutes until the mixture is golden and crunchy.

Turn the oven off and leave the tray of granola inside to cool slowly and dry out further.

Delicious with oat or hemp milk.

Already this'll get the aromas going in the kitchen, as those honeyed smoky caramel notes and that hint of spicy cinnamon warm through.

And this'll up the aroma ante further, as the nuts toast and the flavours mingle. It's worth checking on the tray every 10 minutes or so, partly to check how much it's browning (and maybe give it a stir and turn round the tray to help it do so evenly) and partly just to get a whiff of those seductive smells. Don't the flavours change and develop and deepen with each tray-check?

If you want, you could add dried fruit to the granola once it's cooled. Cranberries or raisins would work well. And it's great served with a dollop of yoghurt and some sliced banana.

And I let the granola steep in the milk for a few minutes, which for me enhances the eating experience.

TOMATO AND COFFEE MUFFINS

Breakfast in a bun, anyone?

With eggs and plenty of fibre from bran, inulin and wholemeal flour, this is a portable breakfast with a bit of get-up-and-go. It's even got a shot of coffee.

A key component for this is the compote that is, in fact, the backbone of my Ratatouille on page 173. It's not a complicated recipe but it takes up a lot of prep and cooking time as the compote concentrates to an intensely flavourful, jammy tomatoey-ness. It's certainly worth the effort, but it seemed like smart cooking to figure out some other recipes that use the same compote, so you can make a bigger batch to employ in a variety of ways in a variety of dishes. A neat bit of culinary thrift.

For other compote dishes, check out
Pasta puttanesca on page 179 and
Tomato compote ketchup on page 261.

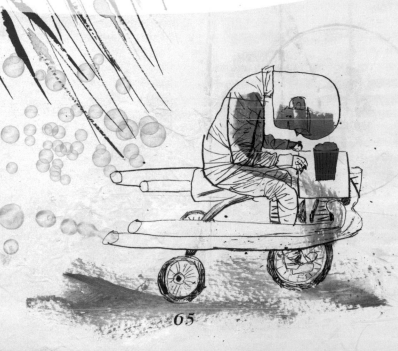

Tomato and Coffee Muffins

MAKES 6

For the tomato coffee mixture
200g Tomato compote (page 174)
1 tsp instant coffee granules

For the muffins
100g unsalted butter, melted
2 large eggs
75g wholemeal flour
50g wheat bran
2 tbsp inulin prebiotic powder (optional)
1 tsp instant coffee granules
1 tsp baking powder
1 tsp salt
Tomato coffee mixture (from above)

Preheat the oven to 200°C/Fan 180°C/Gas 6 and line a muffin tray
with 6 paper muffin cases.

Put the tomato compote into a small pan and add the coffee granules.
Heat gently until the coffee dissolves into the mixture. Spoon 6 heaped
teaspoonfuls of this mixture into a bowl. Leave this and the pan of tomato coffee
mix to cool.

To make the muffins, pour the melted butter into a medium bowl and whisk
in the eggs, one at a time, using a hand mixer.

In a large bowl, mix together the wholemeal flour, wheat bran, inulin powder
if using, coffee granules, baking powder and salt. Make a well in the centre and
add the egg and butter mix. Stir well to combine, then add the tomato coffee mix
from the pan and mix well.

Divide the mixture between the 6 paper cases. Use a teaspoon to make a hollow in
the centre of each muffin and fill each with a heaped teaspoonful of the reserved
tomato coffee mix.

Place on a low shelf in the oven and bake for about 20 minutes until golden and
risen. Transfer to a wire rack to cool.

See how the coffee brings a deeper, darker colour to the mixture. Can you smell some roasted aromas?

Your muffin will contain a little pocket of tomato—coffee jam. You could slice the muffin vertically and spread some on the cut face.

(Or maybe not, if you're on your way to work already.)

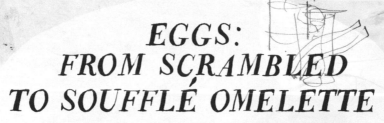

EGGS:
FROM SCRAMBLED
TO SOUFFLÉ OMELETTE

How do you like your eggs?

One of the most complete foods, the egg is an incredible, egg-ceptional thing. We human beings took a big step forward, evolutionarily, once we'd domesticated chickens, which is perhaps why almost every culture in the world has eggs in some form at the centre of their cuisine.

From breakfast to brunch to baking and beyond, eggs are versatile and nutritious. They're also a great opportunity to try out a range of techniques, and to get a real feel for a product and its possibilities.
Are you ready for this?
Then let's crack on...

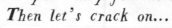

Scrambled

Whisk eggs, milk, cream and melted butter together in a heatproof bowl: for 6 large eggs you could try about 40g butter, 25g milk and 20g crème fraîche, then play around with the ratios until you get the texture you want. Season with salt to taste.

Place the bowl over a pan of simmering **water** (bain-marie) and allow to cook slowly, using a spatula to continuously stir the mixture, cooking until the eggs begin to scramble (this can take up to 20 minutes). Or you can scramble the eggs in a pan over direct low heat, but you'll need to do so very carefully as they can easily and quickly overcook.

Fried

Confit: All Soft
For a completely soft egg, heat enough oil in a saucepan to cover the egg(s). Bring the oil to no higher than 80°C and gently crack the egg in. Cook until the white(s) are opaque.

Sunny Side Up
For a classic sunny side up, heat a small drizzle of oil in a frying pan over a medium-low heat, add the egg(s) and cook until the white is opaque and delicately soft, without colour, and the yolk is still runny.

Over-easy
This allows a more even cook on both sides of the egg. Heat a small drizzle of oil in a frying pan over a medium heat, add the egg(s) and fry until it looks almost cooked then flip over and fry for a little longer. The yolk will be cooked a little more than a sunny side egg.

Crispy
To achieve a crispy texture on the white, heat a generous drizzle of oil in a frying pan over a high heat, add the egg(s) and cook until the white colours. You can choose to flip the egg(s) if you want to but be aware that parts of the yolk will cook firmly over this high heat.

Poached

Heat a pan of salted **water** to no more than 80°C and place a plate upside down in the pan (so that the egg won't come into contact with the hot base and overcook).

Working with one large egg at a time, crack the egg gently into a small bowl or ramekin dish and then gently pour it into a fine-meshed sieve to drain off the watery bits and any stray white; leave to drain for 1–2 minutes.

Using a slotted spoon, carefully collect the egg from the sieve and lower it into the warm **water**. Remove the spoon, leaving the egg to poach for 4 minutes.

Lift the egg out of the **water**, using the slotted spoon, and drain on a plate lined with kitchen paper. Season with salt and freshly ground black pepper.

Once all the eggs are done you can just place them in a pan of warm **water** for 30 seconds or so to warm through.

Some people add vinegar to help set the eggs.
Others find this affects the flavour.
I'm not convinced it's necessary
– especially if you're using very fresh eggs,
which tend to be more homogeneous anyway
– but why not try with and without
a teaspoonful of vinegar to see if you
think it makes a difference?

Continued on next page...

Boiled

This is a tried and trusted technique of mine to achieve soft-boiled eggs. Put the large eggs into a small pan, add enough **water** to cover them and put the lid on the pan. Bring the **water** to a boil over high heat. The moment you see it boiling, take the pan off the heat and set a timer for 6 minutes.

At 6 minutes, remove the egg from the **water** and watch how the **water** evaporates off the shell. This is a great way to judge how hot the shell is and therefore how cooked your egg is. For hard-boiled eggs, allow another couple of minutes.

Basic Omelette

MAKES 1

3 large eggs
25g crème fraîche or soured cream (optional)
50g whole milk (optional)
Salt and white pepper
1 tbsp unsalted butter
Fillings of your choice (such as grated cheese,
sautéed mushrooms, wilted spinach)

In a bowl, whisk the eggs together with the crème fraîche and milk, if using. Season with salt and white pepper.

Melt the butter in a good-quality non-stick omelette pan over a medium heat and allow it to foam and turn nut-brown in colour.

Pour the egg mixture into the pan and use a spatula to keep moving it to the centre every 10 seconds or so; this ensures the uncooked eggs will run into the gaps. Once the mixture starts to resemble scrambled eggs, add your choice of filling.

Leave the omelette in the pan to warm the filling through and to colour and set the egg a little. Use the spatula to fold the omelette in half and transfer it to a warm plate.

French-style Omelette

MAKES 1

For a French-style omelette (which is not dissimilar to scrambled eggs encased by a thin 'skin'), follow the method above but use a much lower heat and do not allow the butter to brown. The eggs will be very soft. This kind of omelette will take longer to cook, about 10 minutes.

Try this method to see what you think.
If, as you're eating, you find yourself
saying 'I'd prefer this more cooked
through' then just leave the eggs in
the water a little longer next time.
A few goes and you'll have the perfect
timing for you.

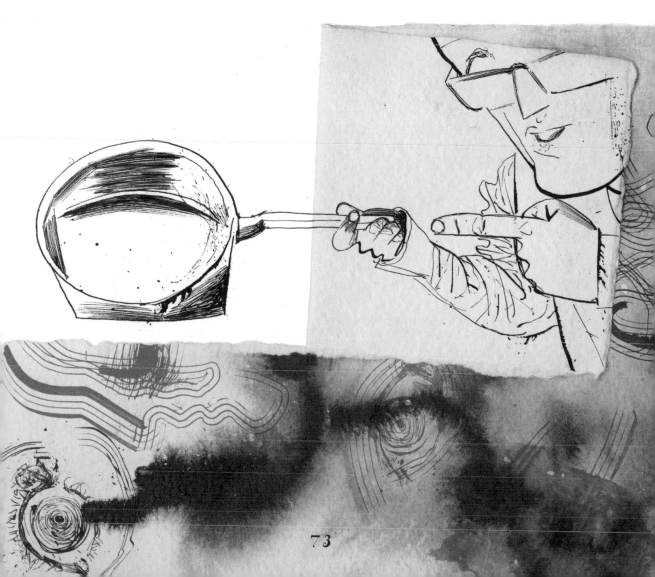

Soufflé Omelette

3 large eggs (preferably older)
1 tsp caster sugar
Salt and white pepper
1 tbsp unsalted butter

For this light, fluffy omelette, separate the eggs, putting the whites into a larger clean bowl, and the yolks into a small bowl.

Add the sugar to the whites and whisk, using a hand mixer, until you achieve soft peaks. Season the egg yolks with salt and ground white pepper, then gently fold into the whisked whites.

Heat the butter in a non-stick frying pan (one that has a well-fitting lid) over a medium heat. Once the butter starts foaming, add the fluffy egg mixture and carefully smooth the surface. Cover with the lid and cook for several minutes, by which time the mixture will have risen slightly and be almost cooked through.

Fold the soufflé omelette in half and leave for a minute to set before transferring it to a warm plate.

'Give us some tips about egg cookery, Heston, please please please.'

'Are you egging me on? OK, there are two key things to bear in mind when cooking eggs.

The first is that an egg changes a lot as it gets older and will behave differently depending on its age.

The freshness of an egg can be the difference between achieving exactly what you want or not. Some recipes – poached or fried, for example – definitely need a young, fresh egg, where the egg white is stronger and there are fewer 'watery' bits. (If you spot watery bits, gently drain the eggs using a sieve before transferring to a ramekin ahead of poaching or frying.)

Meringues, soufflés and omelettes, on the other hand, suit an older egg where the proteins are less strong and elastic and so less likely to prevent the mixture swelling into a nice light airiness.'

Continued on next page...

EGGSPERIMENT:

How do I find out how fresh my egg is?

Fill a bowl with water and place the egg in it.
A very fresh egg will lie on its side.
A less fresh egg will begin to sit upright. The least
fresh will float off the bottom or even to the surface.

Why does this happen?

As the egg ages, it forces the air it contains outwards
where it collects at the rounded end of the shell,
causing the egg to become buoyant and eventually float.

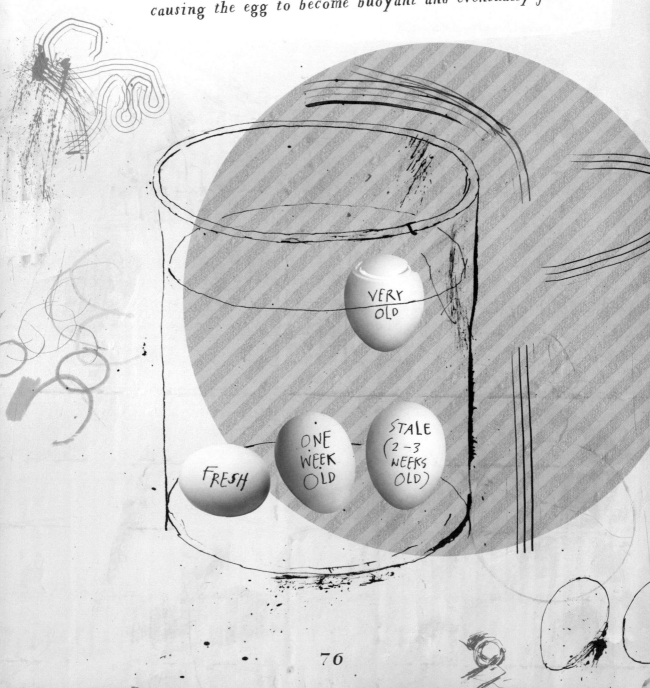

The second thing about eggs to bear in mind is that the white cooks more quickly than the yolk, so the white will be ready when it reaches 68°C whereas the yolk is only ready at 72°C. This means cooking an egg is a balancing act where you want to find the best strategy that'll ensure both white and yolk are set. The recipes here might seem more fiddly or slower than you're used to, but they're designed to pull off that balancing act to perfection.

Finally, a word on storage.
I'd advise *NOT* keeping your eggs
(or your tomatoes, for that matter) in the fridge.
For three good reasons:

1.

A cold egg is more likely to crack in the pan because of the shock of the contrast between hot and cold.

2.

They usually end up stacked in the fridge door, meaning they're jostled every time the door is opened. An egg is a delicate thing that doesn't appreciate rough handling.

3.

An egg can absorb smells very well through its shell. Sit an egg next to a slice of cold pizza and it'll probably take on those aromas, which may not be a flavour combo you're looking for.

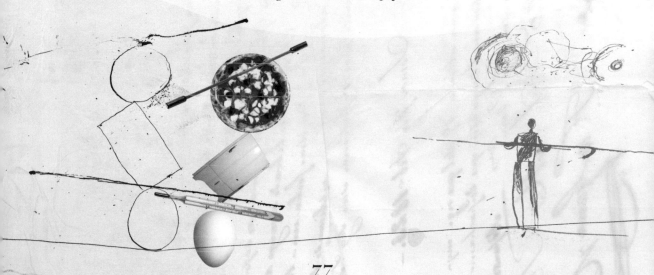

GREEN EGGS AND HAM
Did you read Dr Seuss books as a kid?

I can still remember how, when I was seven, I got a copy of My Book About Me, which had all sorts of categories you could fill in to build up a portrait of yourself. And I did.

My house has ___ windows.
My favourite colour is _____.
There are ___ forks in my house.

I answered them all. On the page headed,

'I like to write stories – here is one I wrote',

I elaborated a narrative about my inventing a spaceship that could 'go anywhere in the universe, even to Ireland'. (I'm not sure if this is an indication of a terrible sense of geography or an enthusiasm for the Emerald Isle as a destination.) The story ended with a solemn, if enigmatic:
'It was good and it was good.'

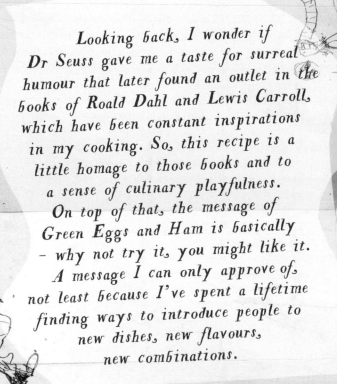

Looking back, I wonder if Dr Seuss gave me a taste for surreal humour that later found an outlet in the books of Roald Dahl and Lewis Carroll, which have been constant inspirations in my cooking. So, this recipe is a little homage to those books and to a sense of culinary playfulness. On top of that, the message of Green Eggs and Ham is basically – why not try it, you might like it. A message I can only approve of, not least because I've spent a lifetime finding ways to introduce people to new dishes, new flavours, new combinations.

Green Eggs and Ham

MAKES 1

For the spinach purée
200g baby spinach leaves
Handful of fresh parsley (about 5g)
Salt

For each green egg
1 medium egg
1 tbsp spinach purée (from above)

To cook and serve
15g unsalted butter (or more if cooking several eggs)
Sliced ham, gammon steak or cooked bacon (optional)

For the spinach purée, bring a large pan of salted **water** to the boil and have a bowl of iced **water** at hand. Add the spinach leaves to the boiling **water** and blanch for 30 seconds only, then remove with a slotted spoon or spider strainer and immediately plunge into the iced **water**. Once cooled, drain the spinach well, squeezing out all excess moisture.

Tip the blanched spinach into a suitable, tall container, add the parsley and use a hand blender to blitz until smooth. Set aside.

To make the green egg(s), carefully separate the egg yolk and white, placing them in separate bowls; set the yolk aside. Add the spinach purée (1 tbsp for each egg) to the egg white and roughly combine using a fork.

To cook, melt the butter in a pan over a medium heat. Spoon the spinach mixture into the pan (in portions, if cooking more than one) and place the reserved yolk in the centre. Cook the egg to your preference. For sunny side up, tilt the pan a little and spoon the hot butter over the green parts.

If you prefer cooked yolks, cook as above, then pop the green egg under a hot grill for 2–3 minutes.

Serve the green egg as it is, or on a slice of warm ham or a gammon steak, or with freshly cooked bacon.

Depending on the size of your pan, you may need to do this in two or three batches, because if you bung too much into a not-so-big pan at once, it will take the water off the boil, preventing you from getting that quick 30-second cook you're looking for. If the spinach is cooked briefly and cooled quickly, it keeps its freshness and its glorious deep-green colour.

This can be done in a clean cloth, but it's just as effective using your hands.
A hands-on moment.
Let's not shy away from mess and ickyness and embrace it like when we were kids.
Get in touch with the tactile.

You'll end up with around 100g purée though you only need 10g per egg.
(A smaller quantity of spinach simply won't blend well.)
But a spinach purée is a delicious thing that can be served as a side, turned into a soup or smoothie, or used as an omelette filling; it also freezes well.

BACON AND EGG PORRIDGE

What do you fancy for
breakfast – Full English?
Bowl of porridge? Kedgeree?

What if you didn't have to choose?
Why not take the eggs, bacon and mushrooms from
the classic British brekkie, the onion and the curry
flavour from the classic Indian dish,
and add it to porridge?
A bold breakfast mash-up.

'Did you know the first Brits in India
developed a taste for kedgeree because
it reminded them of... baby food!'

Bacon and Egg Porridge

SERVES 2

2 tsp vegetable oil, plus extra if needed
4 rashers smoked streaky bacon, chopped
1 small onion, peeled and finely chopped
100g chestnut mushrooms, quartered
400g chicken or vegetable stock
½ tsp curry powder
50g porridge oats
2 tbsp Greek yoghurt
Salt and black pepper
2 boiled or poached eggs (pages 71–2), to serve
Small handful of fresh chives, to finish (optional)

Heat the oil in a large pan, add the bacon and cook until done to your liking.
Remove the bacon using a slotted spoon and set aside, keeping the bacon fat
in the pan.

Reduce the heat to low and add the onion to the pan. Fry gently until softened and
starting to turn golden. Increase the heat to medium and add the mushrooms to the
pan. Cook for another 5 minutes until the mushrooms start to caramelise.
(You could increase the heat for the last minute.)

Add the stock and bring the mixture to a boil, then remove from the heat and
set aside.

Heat a clean, dry pan over a medium heat. Add the curry powder and toast lightly
for about a minute, then add the porridge oats and the warm stock with all its bits.
Bring to a simmer and cook at a steady simmer for about 3 minutes; taste to check
the texture of the porridge.

Remove from the heat and stir in the yoghurt. Taste and adjust the seasoning with
salt and freshly ground black pepper, then divide between two warmed bowls.
Scatter the cooked bacon pieces over the porridge and top with your cooked egg.
Finish, if you like, with a scattering of freshly snipped chives.

At *The Fat Duck*, we sieve the oats we use in Snail Porridge prior to cooking. This removes the finer oat 'dust' that may result in a starchier, thicker porridge. Up to you if you want to do this too. It takes a few seconds but I'd say it gives a nicer texture. Try it both ways and see if you agree.

Sometimes cooking does require pre-planning. The heating of the curry powder and oats will take 4 minutes. If you want your egg ready at the same time, you'll need to factor that into your timetable.

If it doesn't seem cooked through, leave it on the heat a little longer until you're happy.

3

Seven Soups

What do you feel *like eating?*

Exhilarating Green Gazpacho

•

Invigorating Strawberry and Tomato Soup

•

Sunshine in a Bowl

•

Comforting Braised Beef Soup

•

A Cricket Pho for Sharing (and Slurping)

•

Gut-friendly Beetroot Soup

•

Creamy Tomato Soup

1 Monday

2 Tuesday

3 Wednesday

4 Thursday

5 Friday

6 Saturday

7 Sunday

EXHILARATING GREEN GAZPACHO

Looking for something to perk you up?

Green ingredients have a lively and enlivening freshness that I really wanted to capture in a bowl. Essentially, then, this is a glorification of green. And since it's a cold soup it holds on to all those delightful but delicate top notes that are soon driven off by the application of heat.

There's an opportunity, here, to explore the diverse flavour profile of green ingredients, from tarragon's anise and spinach's earthiness to green pepper's slight sulphurousness; the mustardy, pepperiness of watercress; the sharp grassiness of a Granny Smith. Take a sniff. Take a nibble. Think what they might bring to the final flavour – which'll have a depth and complexity because of these diverse characteristics.

Then there's those green tomatoes. Unless you've got hold of one of the striped heirloom varieties, your green tomatoes are basically unripe red. How do you find they differ in texture and flavour? A firmness maybe, and a sharper, tarter, less fruity flavour that'll suit our soup.

'What's the difference between a smoothie and a soup, especially if it's cold? Maybe it's another example of quantum gastronomy. Until you observe it and give it a name, it has the potential to be either.'

'Schrödinger's smoothie, anyone?'

Exhilarating Green Gazpacho

SERVES 2

2 green tomatoes, roughly chopped
180g roughly chopped cucumber
1 Granny Smith apple, roughly chopped
½ green pepper, core and seeds removed, roughly chopped
60g baby spinach leaves
20g watercress leaves
20g fresh tarragon leaves
10g fresh mint leaves
10g fresh dill
2 slices of white bread, torn into smaller pieces

For the olive oil mayonnaise
1 large egg yolk
2 tsp Dijon mustard
2 tsp Chardonnay vinegar
120g olive oil

To finish the soup
50g Olive oil mayonnaise (from above)
4 tsp tarragon vinegar (or white wine vinegar)
1 tsp salt
Few drops of Japanese special sauce 'umamilicious' (page 251)

For the soup base, put all the ingredients into a blender and blitz until smooth. Strain the mixture through a large, fine-meshed sieve into a bowl, pushing the mixture through with the back of a spoon. Cover and chill.

To make the mayonnaise, combine the egg yolk, mustard and wine vinegar in a small bowl. Slowly whisk in the olive oil, a few drops at a time to start with and then in a steady stream, until you have an emulsified mayonnaise.

To finish, put the green soup base into a clean blender and add 50g of the olive oil mayonnaise, the tarragon vinegar and salt. Blitz well to combine then season with a few drops of umamilicious sauce, to taste.

Serve the green gazpacho chilled (ideally in chilled bowls), finished with a swirl of the olive oil mayonnaise if you like.

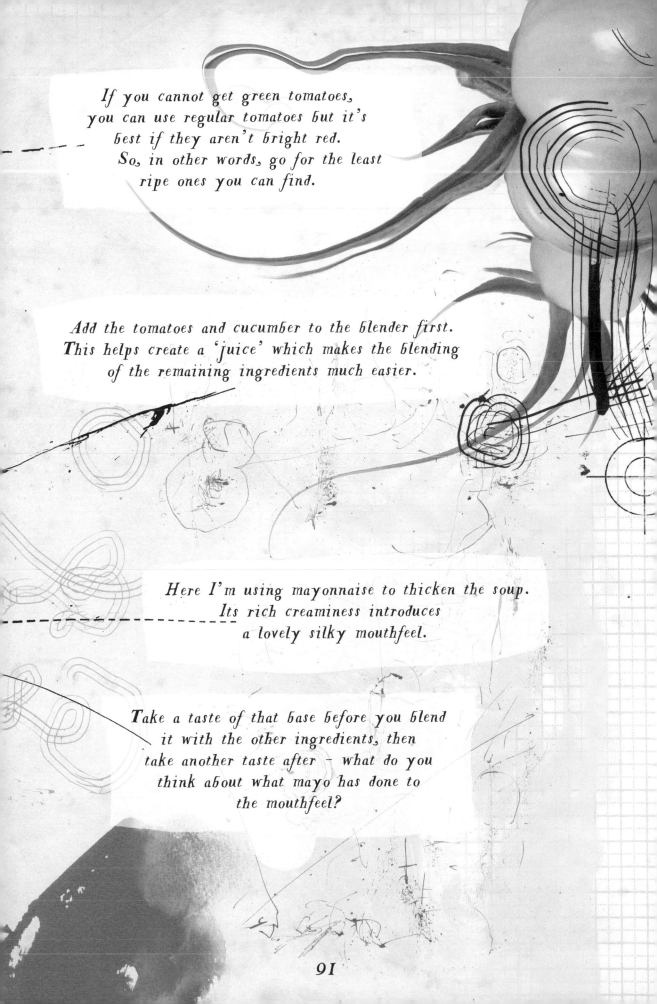

If you cannot get green tomatoes,
you can use regular tomatoes but it's
best if they aren't bright red.
So, in other words, go for the least
ripe ones you can find.

Add the tomatoes and cucumber to the blender first.
This helps create a 'juice' which makes the blending
of the remaining ingredients much easier.

Here I'm using mayonnaise to thicken the soup.
Its rich creaminess introduces
a lovely silky mouthfeel.

Take a taste of that base before you blend
it with the other ingredients, then
take another taste after – what do you
think about what mayo has done to
the mouthfeel?

INVIGORATING STRAWBERRY AND TOMATO SOUP

Have you ever noticed how a blob of tomato pulp looks a lot like a strawberry?

For me, these two can really complement each other, melding to bring depth and flavour complexity to this dish, which has a fresh vitality that'll give you a real re-charge.

You might think they're an odd combination. But, for starters, as you probably know, the tomato is technically a fruit. As are cucumbers, red peppers, courgettes, avocados, green beans, pea pods and pumpkin.

We diligently try to rank, organise and classify the world – decreeing that a fruit is defined as a plant's ovary: its seed container – but the tomato doesn't know it's a fruit and it doesn't care about such distinctions. It just is.

Strawberries, in any case, can pair with a surprising – and surprisingly robust – range of ingredients: balsamic, black pepper, mint, wine, coconut. In the past at *The Fat Duck* I've teamed them with olive and leather purée.

'This is in some ways one of the most quantum dishes in the book, with the flavour flipping intriguingly between strawberry and tomato. A delightful experience.'

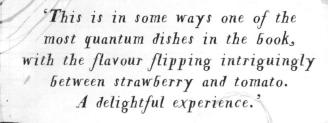

Invigorating Strawberry and Tomato Soup

SERVES 4

1kg fresh or frozen strawberries
1kg chopped plum tomatoes
25g unrefined caster sugar
Finely grated zest of 1 orange
Finely grated zest and juice of 1 lime
12g fresh basil leaves

For the elderflower crème fraîche
75g crème fraîche
2 tsp elderflower cordial
Finely grated zest of ½ lemon

To finish the soup
1 tbsp toasted blanched almonds, chopped
Several fresh basil leaves
Finely grated orange zest
Drizzle of olive oil

To prepare the soup, combine the strawberries, tomatoes, sugar,
citrus zests and lime juice in a bowl. Tear the basil leaves and stir through.
Cover and leave to macerate for at least 2 hours, aggressively stirring
and crushing the mixture after an hour.

Transfer the mixture to a muslin-lined large sieve set over a large bowl.
Leave to strain in the fridge overnight; give the mixture in the sieve a gentle
stir every now and then to help it strain through. You will be left with around
750g bright red, clear soup.

For the elderflower crème fraîche, mix the ingredients together in a bowl until
evenly combined and set aside.

Divide the chilled soup between bowls (preferably chilled) and add a heaped
spoonful of the elderflower crème fraîche to each portion. Garnish with the
chopped, toasted almonds, basil leaves and orange zest. Finish with a drizzle
of olive oil.

Seasonal strawberries are, of course, a pleasure to be treasured.
But frozen strawberries are more convenient for this recipe
as they are effectively partially macerated already.
If you're using fresh strawberries in season,
you'll need to chop them quite small.

To toast the almonds,
spread them out on a small tray
and roast in a preheated oven at
180°C/Fan 160°C/Gas 4 for about 12 minutes until golden.
Roughly chop before using as the garnish.

As an experiment, try crushing one strawberry with
a pinch or two of sugar, and one strawberry without.
Taste each of them and see if you think the sugar
has had any effect on the flavour of the strawberry.
Something mysterious and magical happens
when we combine sugar and fruit.
A sweetened strawberry will seem to have greater
strawberry flavour than an unsweetened one, even though
the actual flavour level stays the same.

Using a wooden spoon will
help crush the cell walls
of the fruit, releasing
more juice and flavour.

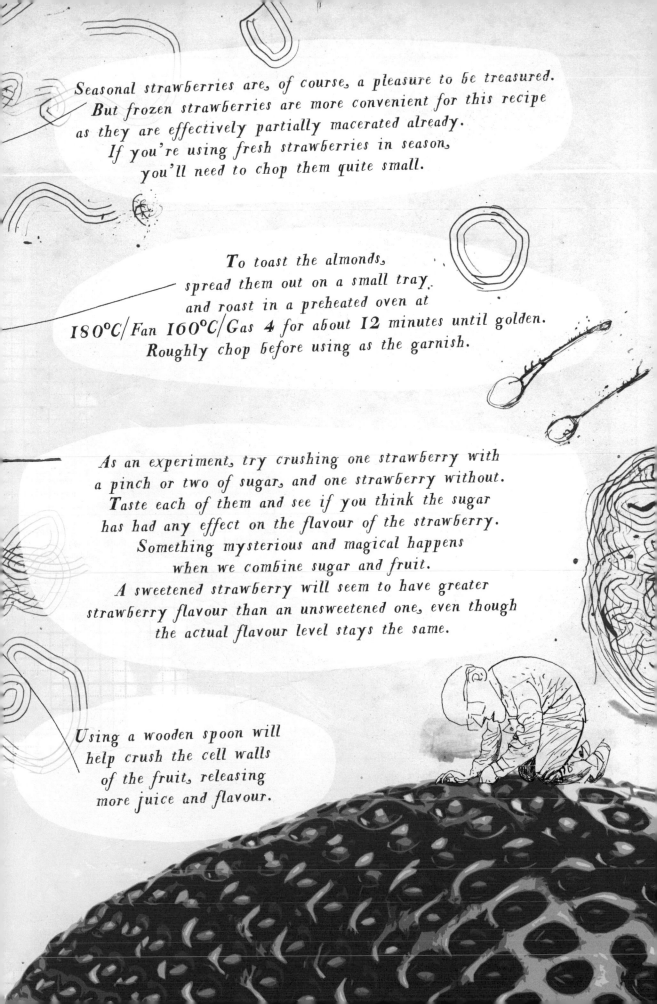

SUNSHINE IN A BOWL
Ready for a Vitamin D spree?

The sun can be a real lift to the spirits, and I began to wonder if I could somehow capture that. Which in turn started me thinking about Vitamin D because the sunshine of the summer months doesn't just enhance our mood, it activates the process by which the body makes Vitamin D, which helps ensure healthy teeth, bones and muscles. What if I created a soup with lots of ingredients that are rich in Vitamin D, such as salmon, mushrooms and oatmeal? Maybe that would offer a rewarding experience, particularly from October to March when, in Britain, we don't make much Vitamin D from sunlight alone, but, of course, you can serve it any time you like.

Sunshine in a Bowl

SERVES 2

For the mushroom purée
500g roughly chopped chestnut mushrooms
40g olive oil
2 sprigs of fresh thyme
1 tbsp dry white wine
2 tsp sherry vinegar
Salt and black pepper

For the soda bread
300g wholemeal flour, plus extra for dusting
50g oatmeal
1 tsp bicarbonate of soda
1 tsp sea salt flakes
½ tsp unrefined caster sugar
20g chilled unsalted butter, diced, plus extra for greasing
200g whole milk

For the cured salmon
10g coriander seeds
½ tsp black peppercorns
20g unrefined caster sugar
75g sea salt flakes
Finely grated zest of 1 lemon and 1 grapefruit
300g skinless salmon fillets

For the fish soup base
1 tbsp olive oil
90g peeled and roughly chopped white onion
40g roughly chopped celery
20g roughly chopped fennel
10 black peppercorns
6 coriander seeds
2 sprigs of fresh thyme
500g fish stock (store-bought is fine)
Few sprigs of fresh parsley
2 tbsp double cream
Finely grated zest of 1 lemon

To finish the soup
3 chestnut mushrooms, thinly sliced
Handful of baby spinach leaves
1 tsp olive oil
½ tsp lemon juice, or more if needed
Small handful of fresh chives
Few drops of Japanese special sauce 'umamilicious' (page 251)
Fresh herbs, to garnish (chives and dill are good options)

With no yeast to coax to life,
and no kneading or rising required,
this has got to be one of the easiest
breads to make.
An excellent introduction to bread-making
that'll still have comforting toasted
aromas wafting up from your oven.

'Curing
the salmon?
So you're
Dr Blumenthal
now?'

'Actually, I am.
But curing here means combining salt, an amount of sugar
(depending on what sweetness level you want)
and some aromatics - in this recipe it's citrus
but you could use spices or herbs. I'm coating
an ingredient in them in order to firm up its
texture and concentrate its flavour
(as salt draws out some of the moisture)
and introduce extra flavours.
It's a very useful process that can
take a fish in an interesting direction.
A technique well worth exploring.'

Continued on
next page...

For the mushroom purée, blitz the mushrooms in a food processor to a purée. Heat the olive oil in a pan over a medium-high heat and add the mushroom purée with the thyme sprigs. Cook for about 15 minutes, stirring regularly to prevent the mixture catching. Reduce the heat and cook until all the moisture has evaporated; this will take around 15 minutes. Add the wine and cook for 2 minutes then remove the pan from the heat. Stir in the sherry vinegar and season with salt and freshly ground black pepper to taste. Pick out and discard the thyme sprigs. Set aside to cool. You will need 200g for the soda bread.

To make the soda bread, preheat the oven to 230°C/Fan 220°C/Gas 8. Butter a 500g (2lb) loaf tin and dust with flour. Combine the flour, oatmeal, bicarbonate of soda, salt and sugar in a large bowl. Add the butter and rub it into the flour using your fingertips, until the mixture resembles coarse breadcrumbs. Make a well in the centre and tip in the 200g mushroom purée and the milk. Mix until evenly combined. Transfer to the prepared tin, cover with foil and bake for 20–25 minutes. Remove the foil and bake for another 20–25 minutes until golden brown. Leave in the tin for 5 minutes then turn out onto a wire rack to cool.

To cure the salmon, toast the coriander seeds in a hot, dry pan until fragrant. Crush the toasted seeds with the peppercorns, using a pestle and mortar, then combine with the sugar, salt and grated citrus zests. Lay the salmon on a tray and scatter the cure mix over all sides. Place in the fridge to cure for 45 minutes.

Brush off and discard the cure mix, then rinse the salmon under cold running water for 5 minutes. Pat dry and set aside. (Or confit if you prefer, see below.)

For the fish soup base, heat the olive oil in a pan and add the onion, celery, fennel, peppercorns, coriander seeds and thyme. Add a pinch of salt and cook over a medium heat until the vegetables are softened, without colour. Pour in the fish stock and simmer for 5–7 minutes until the liquid is reduced a little. Remove from the heat, add the parsley and leave to infuse for 10 minutes only. Pass through a sieve, discarding the vegetables and flavourings. Return to a clean pan and add the cream and lemon zest. Taste and adjust the seasoning with salt and freshly ground black pepper. Keep warm until ready to serve.

To serve, combine the sliced mushrooms, spinach, oil and lemon juice in a bowl. Finely chop the chives and add them too. Season with salt and pepper and gently combine. Divide between two warm soup bowls and top with slices of cured salmon (or flaked pieces, if using salmon confit). Pour over the hot soup and serve with slices of soda bread (toasted if preferred). Add a little more lemon juice and a few drops of umamilicious sauce to taste. Garnish with herbs.

Salmon Confit
If you prefer you can cook the cured salmon confit-style. Put the cured salmon into a sterilised Kilner jar, cutting it into smaller pieces to fit if necessary. Pour in enough olive oil to cover it, leaving at least a 2cm space at the top of the jar. Secure the lid, place the jar in a deep pan and add enough cold water to the pan to come to the same level as the oil in the jar. Lift the jar out and heat the water to 50°C as registered on a temperature probe. Return the jar to the pan for 15 minutes, keeping the water at 50°C. Remove the jar from the water and check the salmon. It should be soft and moist and flake easily.

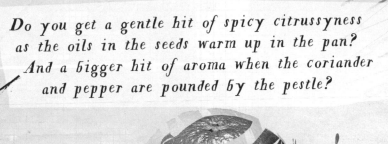

Do you get a gentle hit of spicy citrussyness as the oils in the seeds warm up in the pan? And a bigger hit of aroma when the coriander and pepper are pounded by the pestle?

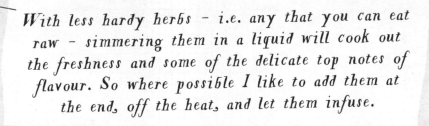

With less hardy herbs – i.e. any that you can eat raw – simmering them in a liquid will cook out the freshness and some of the delicate top notes of flavour. So where possible I like to add them at the end, off the heat, and let them infuse.

COMFORTING BRAISED BEEF SOUP

What food do you turn to for comfort?

How we react to food and how we experience its flavours depends on so much more than just what's going on in our mouth and nose. It's about an emotional response - what memories, what associations are triggered - which is very personal. We can talk about taste receptors and the like but, in the end, there's nothing objective about food and flavour. I love tonka beans for their almost rubbery flavour, which reminds me of beach shoes I wore as a kid when on holiday. A friend of mine hates them for much the same reason: rubber reminds her of the anaesthetic mask at the dentist. No two people perceive and experience a flavour the same way.

So, you may or may not agree with me when I say, this is a bowl of very comforting flavours: beef, bone marrow, red wine, garlic, star anise, mushrooms, root veg, hardy herbs - it's all robust, autumnal, warming, aromatic, indoorsy. At least, those are my associations.

Comforting Braised Beef Soup

SERVES 6

1.5kg beef cheek
2 tsp vegetable oil
Salt and black pepper
200g red wine
2g star anise (about 4)
10g dried shiitake mushrooms
1 litre beef stock
1 litre **water**
180g peeled and roughly chopped onion (1 medium-large)
100g peeled and roughly chopped carrot (1 small-medium)
40g roughly chopped celery (about 1 stalk)
100g quartered mushrooms
15g peeled garlic (about 4 medium cloves), sliced
8 sprigs of fresh thyme
2 fresh or dried bay leaves
3 sprigs of fresh rosemary
5 sprigs of fresh tarragon
Small handful of fresh parsley

For the bone marrow toast
170g bone marrow
1 small shallot, peeled and finely chopped
½ small garlic clove, peeled and crushed
55g dry breadcrumbs
1 anchovy fillet, drained and finely chopped (optional,
but encouraged)
2g finely grated lemon zest
Pinch of salt
Handful of fresh parsley
Small handful of fresh tarragon
Small handful of fresh chervil
6 slices of bread (of your choice)

To braise the beef cheek, select a deep pan large enough to take the beef covered in the braising liquid. Heat 1 tsp oil in the pan over a medium-high heat. Season the beef all over with salt. Add the meat to the pan and colour on all sides, turning as necessary, until dark and golden.

Add the wine, star anise and dried shiitake and cook for about 5 minutes or until the wine is evaporated. Pour in the stock and **water**, making sure the meat is completely covered, and reduce the heat to low. Put the lid on and cook gently for 3–4 hours until the beef is completely tender.

Take the pan off the heat and set aside, leaving the beef in the stock for now.

To prepare the soup, heat 1 tsp oil in a large pan over a medium heat. Add the onion, carrot, celery, mushrooms and garlic, and cook until soft, golden and caramelised. At the same time, carefully lift the braised beef from the stock and place in a bowl; cover with foil and set aside. Tip the caramelised veg into the pan of stock and return it to the heat. Put the lid on and simmer over a medium-low heat for 30 minutes.

In the meantime, make the bone marrow toast. Scoop the marrow from the bone and roughly dice. Place in a bowl with the shallot, garlic, breadcrumbs, anchovy if using, lemon zest and salt. Mix gently to combine and keep in the fridge while you preheat the oven grill to medium-high. Finely chop the herbs (you'll need 5g parsley, 2.5g tarragon and 2.5g chervil) and fold through the mixture.

Toast the bread on both sides, then spread the bone marrow mix on top. Place on the grill rack and grill for about 5 minutes until golden brown.

To finish the soup, tie the thyme, bay, rosemary and tarragon together with string. Remove the pan of soup from the heat, add the herb bouquet and leave to infuse for 5 minutes. Remove and discard the herbs and the star anise.

Pull the beef cheek meat into smaller pieces. Add to the pan and warm through for about 4 minutes. Taste and adjust the seasoning with salt and freshly ground black pepper.

Just before serving, chop the parsley (you need about 1 tbsp) and stir through the soup. Ladle into warmed bowls, top each portion with a bone marrow toast and serve at once.

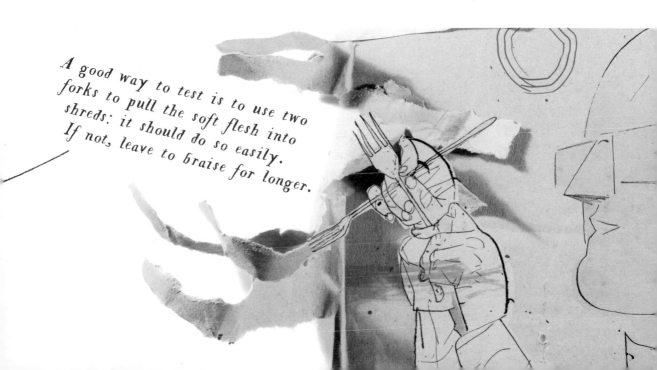

A good way to test is to use two forks to pull the soft flesh into shreds: it should do so easily. If not, leave to braise for longer.

A CRICKET PHO FOR SHARING (AND SLURPING)

Fancy an Asian classic with a twist?

This version of Vietnam's national dish is a great showcase for cricket stock. Traditionally, the melange of broth, noodles and herbs is likely to have beef in it, but I'd say my stock supplies all the robust depth of flavour you need.

In the West, slurping your food is for some reason seen as rude and uncultivated.
In the East, on the other hand, it's not only socially acceptable to slurp a noodle soup, it's considered polite. Why?
Because it shows you're enjoying your food.
What's more, that slurp draws air into the mouth, which helps bring out the flavours.
So, if we ditched prim dining gentility in favour of a noisy exuberance, our soup would actually taste better!

'Hand round the bowls and let's have a slurpathon. Post it on TikTok. Slurp our way to a revolution.'

A Cricket Pho for Sharing (and Slurping)

SERVES 2

1 litre Cricket stock (page 317)
1 small carrot, peeled and finely chopped
1 large onion, peeled and finely chopped
50g peeled and sliced fresh ginger
4 peeled garlic cloves, crushed
1 tbsp coriander seeds
1 small cinnamon stick
3 star anise
6 cloves
20g fish sauce

To assemble the pho
2 portions of rice noodles
1 small courgette, cut into matchsticks
1 small carrot, peeled and cut into small matchsticks
½ spring onion, sliced
1 red chilli, finely sliced
¼ small cucumber, cut into matchsticks
14 fresh coriander leaves
8 fresh mint leaves
6 fresh Thai basil leaves (or regular basil)
Lime wedges, to serve

Combine all the ingredients for the pho, except the fish sauce, in a large pan, bring to a simmer and simmer over a medium-low heat for 15 minutes. Strain through a fine-meshed sieve into a clean pan and stir in the fish sauce.

In the meantime, cook the rice noodles according to the packet instructions.

Divide the cooked, drained noodles between warmed bowls and add the courgette and carrot. Reheat the pho if necessary, then pour into the bowls. Top with the spring onion, chilli, cucumber and herb leaves.

Serve immediately, with lime wedges.

GUT—FRIENDLY BEETROOT SOUP

How about getting friendly with your gut?

A friend of mine read that playing music to your child while in the womb influences the development of their brain. He didn't know if it was true but decided he had nothing to lose and started playing Marvin Gaye's What's Going On a lot.

Maybe we can take a similar approach with the gut. Scientists have established that there's a whole universe inside us, populated by a hundred trillion microbes that have a significant influence not just on our digestion but on our physical and even mental health. The science of the microbiome is in its infancy so we don't yet know the whole story, but it seems to me we've got little to lose by exploring what foods might benefit the gut and its microbial residents.

So, this soup is structured around beetroot, barley and kefir, all of which appear to have beneficial effects on our digestive health. There's lots of beetroot in the recipe because it's got plenty of fibre, it's an anti—inflammatory and it contains lots of glutamine, an amino acid that's good for gut maintenance.

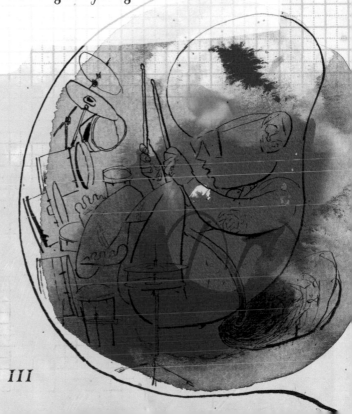

Gut-friendly Beetroot Soup

SERVES 2

For the pickled beetroot
70g white wine vinegar
80g peeled beetroot, finely chopped

For the beetroot stock
2 tbsp vegetable oil
2 small onions, peeled and finely sliced
½ garlic clove, peeled and crushed
150g peeled beetroot, thinly sliced
3 litres **water** (or vegetable stock)
Salt and black pepper

For the beetroot barley
2 tbsp vegetable oil
100g peeled shallots, finely chopped
100g pearl barley, well rinsed and drained
750g beetroot stock (from above)
150g peeled beetroot, grated

For the pan-roasted root vegetables
2 tbsp vegetable oil
150g peeled root vegetables (your favourite),
cut into 1cm dice

For the kefir horseradish
50g kefir
15g creamed horseradish
1 tsp white wine vinegar
Few sprigs of fresh dill

To finish the soup
Handful of fresh dill,
plus extra sprigs to garnish
250g beetroot stock (from above)
30g peeled beetroot, grated

For the pickled beetroot, bring the wine vinegar to the boil in a small pan and add the beetroot. Immediately take the pan off the heat and leave the beetroot to cool and pickle for 2 hours. Drain before using: you need 80g for the soup.

To make the beetroot stock, heat the oil in a large pan and add the onions and garlic. Cook over a medium heat until softened. Add the beetroot and continue to cook until the mixture starts to caramelise. Pour in the **water** (or stock) and simmer for 45 minutes. Strain the stock and adjust the seasoning with salt and freshly ground black pepper. You need 750g for the barley; 250g to finish the soup.

If you are also making the pan-roasted vegetables at this point, add all their peelings and trimmings into the stock pan at the same time as the water. Less waste, extra flavour.

PROTEIN

Continued on next page...

For the beetroot barley, heat the oil in a large pan over a medium heat,
then add the shallots and cook gently until softened.
Add the pearl barley, increase the heat and let it toast a little.
Pour in the beetroot stock, add the grated beetroot and reduce the heat to a simmer.
Cook for 25–30 minutes until the barley is tender; you need about 400g.
Adjust the seasoning with salt and freshly ground black pepper.

For the pan-roasted vegetables, heat the oil in a pan over a medium-high heat.
Add the diced vegetables and cook until evenly coloured on all sides.
Transfer to a tray lined with kitchen paper to drain and season with salt
and freshly ground black pepper.

To make the kefir horseradish, combine the kefir, creamed horseradish and wine
vinegar in a bowl and season with salt to taste. Just before serving, finely
chop the dill (you need about 1 tsp) and stir through the mixture.

To finish the soup, warm the beetroot barley through in a large pan over a medium
heat. Finely chop the dill (you need 1 tbsp) and stir through. In a separate pan,
bring the beetroot stock to a simmer and add the roasted vegetables, the
80g pickled beetroot and the grated beetroot. Simmer for 2 minutes, then strain
through a sieve, saving the roasted vegetables and beetroot.

To serve, spoon the beetroot barley into the centre of two warmed bowls and pour
on the stock. Divide the roasted vegetables and beetroot between the bowls, spoon
the kefir horseradish into the centre and garnish with sprigs of dill.

Toasting a grain adds an extra flavour dimension,
introducing complex Maillard flavours.
(Think coffee, chocolate and bread crust:
these are all the result of Maillard reactions.)
I like to toast risotto rice in the same way,
just to add a layer of flavour complexity.

The barley~beetroot mix will
seem more wet than a risotto.
Don't fret the wetness.

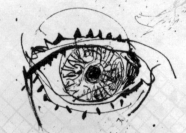

Three ingredients with an invigorating sharpness.
Taste the kefir: doesn't it have tangy,
tart even sour taste? As for horseradish:
what about that pungent, mustardy, sinus~clearing
kick it has? Does it bring tears to your eyes?

Creamy Tomato Soup

Does tomato soup trigger nostalgia when you cook it?

I'd definitely say that, as I stir the saucepan on the hob, it stirs up memories. Maybe it's just because I had a lot of Heinz cream of tomato when I was a kid, particularly if I was getting over an illness. But there's just something emotional and transporting about a bowl of the orange–red stuff. (Did you use to drizzle a swirl of milk or cream into it?)

Of course, you might say, if I want a shot of nostalgia, why don't I just buy a can? After all, that's exactly what I had when I was young so what can be more nostalgic than that? And there's a lot of truth in that. In my cooking I've spent a lot of time re–exploring dishes that I loved as a child, and sometimes I've tried to 'improve' the ingredients only to find that, in doing so, I'd somehow removed the real heart of the dish. In more than one of my retro reinventions I've tested out all kinds of wonderful bread before realising that only bog–standard sliced white will do. (Sometimes nostalgia is exactly what it used to be.)

Here, though, I find that this soup is richly, silkily, smoothly and sweetly delicious in its own right, and still manages to provoke nostalgia and a feeling of comfort.

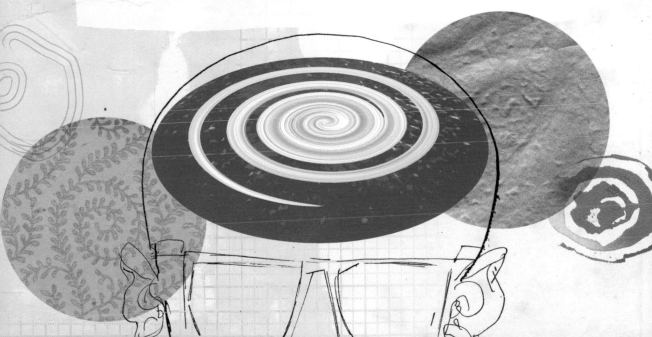

Creamy Tomato Soup

SERVES 4

2kg vine tomatoes
100g unsalted butter
Olive oil for cooking, plus a trickle to serve
½ onion, peeled and finely sliced
4 garlic cloves, peeled and finely chopped
1 celery stalk, chopped
9–10 sprigs of fresh thyme
2 tbsp tomato ketchup
200g double cream
Salt and black pepper
Extra virgin olive oil, to finish

Halve the tomatoes and scoop out the seeds, placing the seeds in a sieve set over a bowl to strain the juices. Chop the tomato flesh into smaller pieces.

Melt half the butter with a little olive oil in a large pan over a medium heat. Add the onion and garlic and cook for 5 minutes to soften. Add the celery, chopped tomatoes along with the strained juices, thyme and ketchup. Increase the heat and bring to the boil, then reduce to a simmer. Cook until the liquid is reduced by two-thirds; this can take up to an hour.

Pick out and discard the thyme then transfer the mixture to a blender and blitz until smooth. Pass through a fine-meshed sieve into a clean pan. Add the cream and heat through gently. Whisk in the remaining butter and season with salt and freshly ground black pepper.

Divide the soup between warmed bowls and finish with a trickle of olive oil.

Often, the seeds and pulp just get discarded. But I'm one of the authors of a scientific paper with the catchy title 'Differences in Glutamic Acid and 5'-Ribonucleotide Contents between Flesh and Pulp of Tomatoes and the Relationship with Umami Taste', which details how that pulp has a high concentration of umami. A simple straining of the seeds lets you add in extra savoury flavour.

When you reduce, you're driving off water, which will make the soup less dilute and so help intensify the flavour, giving it that totally terrific tomatoeyness we're looking for.

4

A Composed Salad

Why did the tomato blush?

Salad-making

•

A Macerated Salad

•

Barbecue Vegetable Salad

•

Beetroot and Pea Salad

•

Quinoa with Vegetables

•

Hedgerow Salad

•

Salad Dressings

'So why did the tomato blush?'

'Because it saw the salad dressing, of course.'

'Talking of which, have you got any tips about salad-making for me, Big H?'

'Well, you can have a salad as a starter, a side, a main, after the main (very French) or as a dessert.'

'Huh?'

'Fruit salad.'

'Oh, yeah. And you could even have it as a sandwich – like our Pan bagnat on page 49 or our Prawn cocktail salad sandwich on page 41.'

'Even the name isn't much help. The word "salad" comes from the Latin for "salted greens" so I guess, here's my tip: get yourself some leaves. Little Gem lettuce, rocket, watercress, spinach, pea shoots, or whatever. Or a mix of these. Dress them in a vinaigrette. Season. Job done.'

'Whoa, whoa, whoa. There's got to be more to it than that.'

'Has there? Sometimes that's exactly what I want: the freshness of a green leaf or two coated in smooth fruity olive oil and a little kick of vinegar. But if you're looking for a guide, don't ask me, ask yourself. Ask your gut. What do I want to eat? What do I feel like eating?'

'Because food is about emotion and imagination?'

'Well said. Perhaps you're not as green as you're cabbage-looking.'

'I hope you're not going to spend the rest of this conversation thinking up food-based puns.'

'OK. Before I get a dressing down (that's the last, I promise!), what do you want? A veg or two to add flavour and texture and variety?'

Continued on next page...

'Like tomatoes or char-grilled asparagus or sweetcorn or spring onions or griddled courgettes or cucumber or beetroot or mushrooms or green beans or petits pois...'

'Is it going to be a meal in itself rather than a side? Maybe you want more bulk and body?'

'Goat's cheese, tuna, quinoa, boiled potatoes, hard-boiled eggs...'

'Now you're cooking.
(Oops. That really is the last one.)
Do you want some pops and punches of flavour in there?'

'Capers, gherkins, olives, anchovies, pickled onion, pickled beetroot, pickled lemon...'

'A touch more texture for crunch and contrast?'

'Crispy onions, cobnuts, pumpkin seeds, toasted cumin...'

'Plus, perhaps, a fragrant top note for freshness and complexity?'

'Thyme, mint, coriander, basil...'

'Of course, you've just chosen ingredients from the recipes overleaf...'

'Rumbled!'

124

'But this is just the tip of the iceberg (lettuce). There are countless other ingredients in each of those categories – leaves, extra flavour, texture, punch, freshness, body – which might bring something stimulating and satisfying to your salad. There are days when you might just crave a few leaves. Or a salad with no leaves, like potato or carrot or a caprese. As I said, you've just got to ask yourself, what do I feel like eating today? Follow your gut and your gut feeling. Follow your taste and flavour memories. Use your imagination.'

A MACERATED SALAD

So, when it comes to salad-making, there really are no rules.

An illustration of this is a salad I made a while back, which I dressed but then put in the fridge and forgot about. Kitchen lore has it that a dressed salad needs to be eaten straight away, before it becomes limp and disappointing. But when I tasted mine a couple of days later, I thought it had an interesting, almost pickled character that I liked a lot. And so, the macerated salad was born. Another example of how, in cooking, we should question everything.

If you want to try it out, round up a selection of tomatoes, lettuce, cucumber, spring onions and olives, or whatever you have to hand. Dice them and toss with a Classic vinaigrette (page 146). Cover and leave in the fridge overnight, and observe how the flavour and texture changes as the elements start to pickle.

BARBECUE VEGETABLE SALAD

Isn't there something special about cooking over an open fire?

Of course, it's a signal of summer and a seductive sensory experience – the warmth of the sun and the barbecue on your face, the waft of those lovely char-grilled aromas scenting the air and making the mouth water.

But maybe it's more hard-wired than that. Scientists are still debating when we first learned to control fire, but once we did we were enabled to eat a far wider range of foods and thus take in more calories, which was important for the development of the human brain because it's a calorie-hungry organ.

(The fact that our teeth and digestive tract got smaller at the same time as our ancestors' brains expanded suggests a strong link between diet and the brain's evolution.) The combination of food and fire made we humans what we are.

Maybe that's why we are all drawn towards the ritual of the barbecue and flames. Usually we associate it with great slabs of meat, but in fact char-grilling adds real character to vegetables too. So why not grab some veg and go release your inner caveman or woman?

Barbecue Vegetable Salad

2 corn-on-the-cob
1 courgette, halved lengthways
1 red pepper, core and seeds removed
100g spring onions, trimmed
½ cucumber, halved lengthways
2 Little Gem lettuce, halved lengthways
250g cherry tomatoes on-the-vine
4 tbsp olive oil
Salt and black pepper
2 tbsp oak smoking chips (optional)
1 tbsp wholegrain mustard
2 tbsp sherry vinegar
1–2 tbsp store-bought crispy onions, to finish

Light your barbecue and allow the coals to cook down until they have a fine coating of ash.

Place all the vegetables and the cherry tomatoes in a large bowl and drizzle over the olive oil. Season with salt and toss gently until evenly coated. Take out the tomatoes and set aside.

You will need to cook the vegetables on the barbecue in batches, starting with the corn since it will take the longest and following with the courgette and red pepper, then the spring onions, cucumber and lettuce. As the vegetables are cooked, remove them from the barbecue and place on a large tray.

Scatter the smoking chips, if using, over one area of the coals, then place the cherry tomatoes on the rack over this area and cook until blackened on all sides then remove and add to the tray.

Chop the courgette, red pepper, spring onions, cucumber and lettuce into smaller chunks and place in a large bowl. Strip the corn kernels from the cobs by running a sharp knife down the sides of each cob, then add them to the bowl.

To dress the salad, add the mustard and sherry vinegar and toss well to coat evenly. Taste and adjust the seasoning with salt and freshly ground black pepper.

Take the cherry tomatoes off their vine and tumble them through the salad. Serve scattered with the crispy onions for a crunchy finish.

Delicious as a side salad with a simple barbecued or grilled piece of meat or fish.

This is a relaxing way to cook.
In the open air, nudging each ingredient around
on the grill till it's done then replacing it with another.
A gentle culinary rhythm. A time for pleasurable
sensory observation.

You'll see and smell how different vegetables respond
to heat in different ways.

The corn releasing a sweetness into the air.
The courgettes getting that enticing char-grilled striping.
There's no pressure here – your vegetables are supposed
to blacken and char in places, this is what brings flavour.
You'll notice many of them sag as they soften to readiness.

Which vegetable smells best to you as it chars?
Maybe the spring onions, or the cucumber as it begins
to look and even taste like courgette.

This'll be quick, so keep an eye on the tomatoes
and don't worry if they burst.
Those juices will add flavour to the dressing.

'There's an art to barbecuing that soon falls into place with
experience and a bit of awareness. Placing your hands over
the barbecue and feeling where the hotter and colder spots are
will give you a sense of where to place food depending on
how fast or slow it's cooking. Follow your instincts, follow
your senses, move stuff around as you need to.'

BEETROOT AND PEA SALAD

How about a salad with some green summery freshness, sweetness and earthiness?

Goat's cheese and beetroot is a classic combination
of richness and earthiness that balances beautifully.
Add gently acidic, textured onion slices, sweet peas,
minty herbiness, green leaves and some seeds for crunch
and you've got a salad with all the building blocks in place.

Beetroot and Pea Salad

SERVES 4

2–3 small-medium beetroot
70g red wine vinegar, plus 2 tbsp for the onion
Sea salt
40g peeled and thinly sliced red onion
Pinch of unrefined caster sugar
120g petits pois (defrosted if frozen)
Small handful of fresh mint
Olive oil, to drizzle
20g pumpkin seeds
80g baby spinach
50g pea shoots
80g goat's cheese, sliced

Peel and halve the beetroot and place in a single layer in a small pan. Add the 70g wine vinegar then pour on enough **water** (at least 200g) to cover the beetroot. Season with a pinch of salt and bring to a simmer.

Cook over a medium-high heat until the beets are tender, yet firm, topping up with a little more **water** if needed. Transfer the beetroot to a bowl of iced **water** to cool quickly. Drain well and slice thinly before using.

While the beetroot are simmering, put the thinly sliced red onion into a small bowl and drizzle over the 2 tbsp wine vinegar. Add a small pinch each of salt and sugar. Toss well and leave to pickle for at least 1 hour. (You can do this the evening before if you like and leave it, covered, in the fridge to pickle.)

Tip the petits pois into a bowl. Pick the mint leaves off their stems and chop them finely then add to the peas with a generous drizzle of olive oil. Season with a little salt and gently combine.

Toast the pumpkin seeds in a hot, dry pan until they pop, colour and release their aroma. Remove and set aside to cool.

To assemble, scatter the spinach and pea shoots over a large serving platter and spoon on the minty peas. Arrange the sliced beetroot and goat's cheese on top.

Use a fork to lift the pickled red onion from the bowl and scatter the onion slices over the salad. Finish with a drizzle of olive oil and the toasted pumpkin seeds.

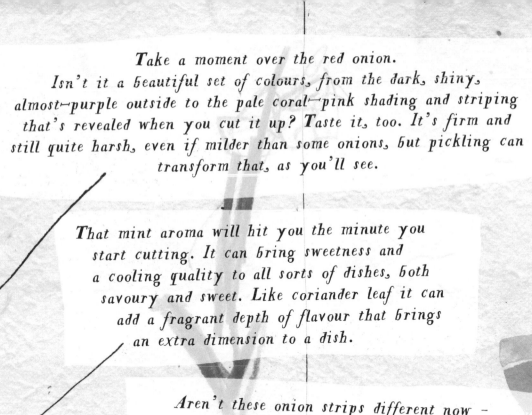

Take a moment over the red onion.
Isn't it a beautiful set of colours, from the dark, shiny, almost-purple outside to the pale coral-pink shading and striping that's revealed when you cut it up? Taste it, too. It's firm and still quite harsh, even if milder than some onions, but pickling can transform that, as you'll see.

That mint aroma will hit you the minute you start cutting. It can bring sweetness and a cooling quality to all sorts of dishes, both savoury and sweet. Like coriander leaf it can add a fragrant depth of flavour that brings an extra dimension to a dish.

Aren't these onion strips different now - softer in structure and less harsh in flavour? But with enough bite- in both senses - to add a contrast to the other ingredients.

This simple little pickled onion could be your secret weapon for so many salads, adding texture, sharpness and acidity.

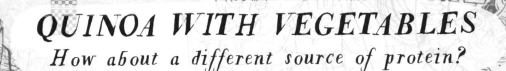

QUINOA WITH VEGETABLES

How about a different source of protein?

A staple part of the Incan and Aztec diet, quinoa is one of those ancient grains that has recently been rediscovered. A few years ago, most of us wouldn't have known how to pronounce it. Now packets are readily available on most supermarket shelves.

Part of the reason for its sudden popularity is the huge number of health benefits packed into this pseudo-cereal. It's gluten-free, making it a good alternative to starchy grains. It's a prebiotic that's good for the gut because it enhances the diversity of beneficial gut bacteria. It's high in fibre, vitamins and minerals, and has a high level of protein. It's also a 'complete protein' as it contains all nine of the essential amino acids our body needs, which is particularly valuable if you're vegetarian or vegan.

All of which is pretty impressive for something the size of a pinhead.

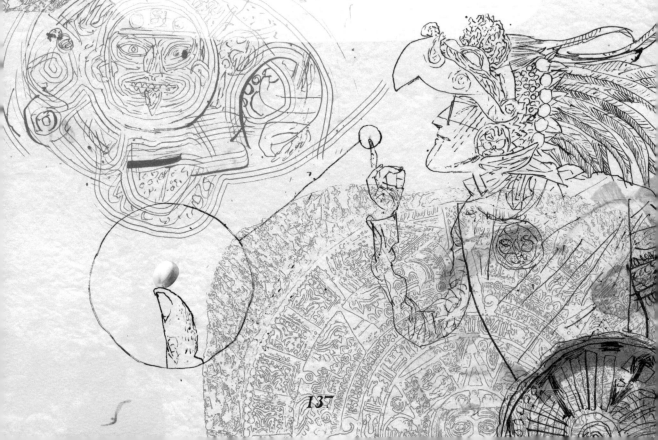

Quinoa with Vegetables

SERVES 6–8

For the semi-dried tomatoes
200g cherry tomatoes, halved
4–5 sprigs of fresh thyme, leaves picked
Pinch of unrefined caster sugar
Pinch of salt

For the quinoa
400g quinoa
1.2 litres vegetable stock
Salt and black pepper
½ red onion, peeled and thinly sliced

For the dressing
300g mayonnaise
Juice of 1½ limes (other lime half saved)
1½ tsp honey
Pinch of cayenne pepper
Pinch of ground cumin
Handful of fresh coriander

For the salad
2 Little Gem lettuce
Handful or two of wild rocket
Cooked vegetables, such as char-grilled asparagus
Other ingredients that could add bursts of flavour, like capers,
gherkins, toasted cumin seeds, pickled lemon

To semi-dry the tomatoes, preheat the oven to 90°C/Fan 70°C/Gas lowest.
In a bowl, toss the cherry tomatoes with the thyme leaves, sugar and salt
to coat then put, cut side up, on a baking tray lined with baking paper.
Place in the oven for 1 hour.

Meanwhile, soak the quinoa in cold **water** for 15–20 minutes, then drain.
In a large pan, bring the stock to the boil. Add the quinoa and simmer for
12–15 minutes or until it is cooked and the stock is all absorbed. Season with
salt and freshly ground black pepper and set aside to cool.

Put the sliced red onion into a small bowl, cover with cold **water** and leave to
soak for 5 minutes. Drain well and stir into the quinoa.

For the dressing, combine the mayonnaise, lime juice, honey, cayenne and cumin in
a bowl. (Keep the other lime half; you may want it later.) Finely chop the coriander
and stir through the dressing. Season with salt and freshly ground black pepper.

Stir three-quarters of the dressing and the semi-dried tomatoes through the quinoa.
Build your salad, adding the lettuce, rocket, cooked veg and whatever elements you
fancy that'll bring flavour, contrast and texture to the dish. If you feel the salad
needs it, drizzle over the remaining dressing and add a squeeze of lime.

Some leaves are always good for colour and freshness: I'm going with *Little Gem* lettuce for crispness, plus sharp, peppery rocket. Asparagus adds a smoky, char-grilled note.
Perhaps I'll reinforce that with a toasted note, by dry-frying some cumin seeds briefly in a pan till their aroma rises.
Something sharp, acidic could be good – gherkins or pickled lemon – to balance the mayo richness. Or perhaps some real pops of acidity from a scattering of capers.
That dressed, tomatoey quinoa base gives you a great foundation for playing around.

Isn't there something satisfying about seeing those halved tomatoes lined up neatly on the tray.
Don't know what it is –
the chef's sense of order perhaps.
Enjoy the herbal aroma that clouds round the kitchen as they gently cook, too, developing that slight crust on the surface.

A lovely nutty, almost buttery, aroma arises as it cooks. You'll know when it's ready by testing it for softness between your teeth. But the quinoa will give you a hint anyway as a sort of curl of white should emerge, like a tiny tail, when it's ready.

HEDGEROW SALAD

Fancy a forage?

Actually, I have to admit, I have misgivings about foraging, which were summed up perfectly by my friend the late, great food writer, A.A.Gill, who once went on a foraging excursion in Australia with another great food-writer friend of mine, Harold McGee. Upon his return, Adrian described the trip as 'a hot walk with flies' and foraging as the process of picking something off a bush and saying, 'Here, taste this – it's like rosemary but not as nice.'

At the same time, there's something to be said for connecting more with the natural world. One of the dishes at The Fat Duck, 'A Walk in the Woods', is inspired by the Japanese ritual of shinrin-yoku: taking a mindful walk in a forest, which can apparently have positive effects on both body and mind. Being more aware of ourselves and the planet and the interplay between the two, with each potentially helping sustain the other, is a form of interconnectedness that can only be beneficial, it seems to me.

So, if you want to go wild, this is a dish you could build from what you find in the countryside. Or you can just see it as a composition symbolic of the natural world, a timely reminder of things that grow out of the earth or the hedges, or fall from the trees. Where our food actually comes from.

Hedgerow Salad

SERVES 2

For the pickled beetroot
5 small-medium beetroot, peeled
1 tsp vegetable oil
Salt
50g olive oil
50g red wine vinegar

For the blackberry dressing
100g blackberries
1 tbsp **water**
2 tsp lemon juice
¾ tsp salt
1½ tsp wholegrain mustard
2 tsp red wine vinegar
25g olive oil
15g pickling liquid (from the beetroot)

To assemble the salad
10 blackberries, halved
2 generous handfuls of salad leaves (of your choice)
4 chestnut mushrooms, thinly sliced
12 peeled cobnuts or hazelnuts, toasted

For the pickled beetroot, preheat the oven to 160°C/Fan 140°C/Gas 3. Cut each peeled beetroot into quarters and toss in the oil and a pinch of salt to coat evenly. Place on a small baking tray, cover tightly with foil and bake for 35–40 minutes or until tender (i.e. when a knife inserted into one meets with no resistance). Return the tray, uncovered, to the oven and cook until the beetroot dry out and become a little sticky. The whole process could take around 45–55 minutes. Set aside to cool.

In a small jug, combine the olive oil, wine vinegar and a generous pinch of salt. Put the cooled roast beetroot into a Kilner jar or other sealable non-reactive container, add the oil and vinegar mixture and leave to pickle in the fridge for at least a day.

For the dressing, put the blackberries into a pan with the **water**, lemon juice, salt, mustard and wine vinegar and cook over a medium-low heat until the berries completely break down, 5–10 minutes. Take off the heat and crush, using the back of a fork. (Or blitz to a purée using a stick blender.) Let cool, then measure 50g.

To finish the dressing, in a bowl, whisk the 50g blackberry purée with the olive oil and 15g pickling liquid from the beetroot.

To assemble the salad, drain the pickled beetroot and combine with the fresh blackberries and salad leaves in a large bowl. Add a little dressing (about 1 tbsp) and toss to coat. Fold in the mushrooms and divide between two bowls or plates. Scatter over the toasted nuts and drizzle with more dressing as needed.

Foraged leaves include sorrel, spinach, dandelion, wild garlic leaves and watercress. Alternatively, use your favourite salad leaves, looking for a nice contrast of flavours and texture. Iceberg, Cos and Little Gem lettuce are fresh, crunchy and light, while rocket and watercress are more peppery. Radicchio and chicory have a brisk bitterness. Spinach and mâche are soft and sweet.

To toast the nuts, spread them out on a small baking tray and place in the oven preheated to 180°C/Fan 160°C/Gas 4 for 12 minutes until golden. Tip the toasted nuts onto a plate and leave to cool.

As the berries warm up, you'll begin to smell a sweet fruitiness that's very different from beetroot's, but you can probably already imagine how the two might complement one another. If the seeds of the blackberry bother you, you can cook as directed but without the wholegrain mustard, then pass the mixture through a sieve before stirring in the mustard.

SALAD DRESSINGS

There are some things – rustling up an omelette; making a sauce for pasta; baking a loaf – that are just cool to be able to do for people. Composing a salad dressing is one of these, and the beauty of it is, first, that it's a versatile skill. Yes, the obvious use is to unite and bring a little piquancy to a bowlful of leaves, but you can also use it to dress crushed potatoes or steamed vegetables, or to liven up cooked pulses, or to drizzle over fish, or even as a marinade for meat.

Second, you can take the classic vinaigrette in almost any culinary direction you can think of, so it's a brilliant opportunity for exploration and experimentation. I'll show you some here, but these are just a start. Once you've got the idea, it's yours to run with – you can, for example, alter the classic 3:1 oil/acid ratio for added sharpness or a mellower dressing. Or change the type of oil or vinegar you use, introducing rice vinegar and ginger for an Asian vibe, replacing vinegar with lemon juice for a fresher, more Mediterranean feel, and so on.

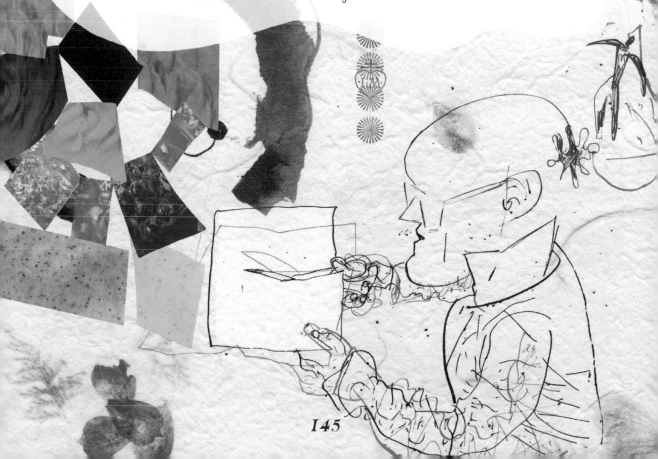

Classic Vinaigrette

Rich, smooth, sharp and with a hint of flavour, this is the workhorse of the salad scene. A go-to dressing for greenery and for steamed vegetables, and a great foundation for any style of dressing you want to make.

MAKES ABOUT 435G

100g Chardonnay vinegar
10g Dijon mustard
300g grapeseed oil
25g warm **water**

Whisk the wine vinegar and mustard together in a bowl or jug. Slowly drizzle in the oil, whisking as you do so, until the dressing is completely emulsified. Finally, whisk in the warm **water**. (Adding a little warm **water** makes the dressing gentler on the palate.)

Mustard Vinaigrette

Adding a little honey gives this a milder, slightly sweeter character than the Classic vinaigrette.

MAKES ABOUT 265G

235g Classic vinaigrette (see above)
25g wholegrain mustard
1 tsp honey (optional)

Whisk the wholegrain mustard, and honey if using, into the vinaigrette.

Shallot and Caper Vinaigrette

With plenty of sharpness and texture from the capers and shallots, this dressing is excellent in leafy salads or potato salads; it also goes well with grilled fish or drizzled over steak tartare or carpaccio.

MAKES ABOUT 135G

100g Classic vinaigrette (see above)
25g drained capers, chopped
10g peeled shallots, finely chopped

Stir the chopped capers and shallots into the vinaigrette.

Asian-style Vinaigrette

With its sweet, sour and umami characteristics, this is a fantastic way of bringing strong, evocative Asian flavours to a dish. Toss something like green beans, edamame beans and broccoli into it to create an Asian-style salad. Or you can use it to marinate meat prior to cooking.

This dressing might look very different from the previous ones, but if you glance at the ingredients, you'll see that underpinning it is a combination of oil and vinegar (though in more of a 2:1 ratio).

MAKES ABOUT 190G

35g seasoned rice vinegar
20g apple cider vinegar
15g light soy sauce
10g honey
100g toasted sesame oil
½ peeled garlic clove, finely chopped
10g peeled and grated fresh ginger
Salt and black pepper
Pinch of dried chilli flakes (optional)

In a bowl, whisk the rice vinegar, cider vinegar, soy sauce and honey together. Slowly drizzle in the sesame oil, as you continue to whisk, until the dressing is completely emulsified. Stir in the garlic and ginger and season with salt and freshly ground black pepper to taste. A pinch of chilli flakes is a great addition if you want some heat.

Yoghurt Dressing

Smooth and tangy from the yoghurt, fresh from the mint, fragrant from the dill, sharp from lime and with a kick of heat from the chilli, this is a great dressing for Greek-style salads but it can also double up as a dip for crudités. It is also lovely with smoked salmon, mackerel or haddock. It can even be used in tacos or burritos or to marinate chicken for a chicken-based curry.

MAKES ABOUT 225G

150g Greek yoghurt
50g semi-skimmed milk
1 tsp lime juice
10g fresh mint
10g fresh dill
1g smoked chilli flakes
Sea salt

Whisk together the yoghurt, milk and lime juice. Finely chop the mint and dill and stir through the mixture, adding a pinch of chilli flakes and salt to season.

Herb Dressing

A rich, thick dressing with plenty of body, this makes an interesting alternative to mayonnaise for salads and sandwiches. It also makes a great sauce for drizzling over smoked salmon.

MAKES ABOUT 175G

½ peeled garlic clove, finely chopped
2 anchovy fillets, drained
10g mayonnaise
115g Greek yoghurt
10g fresh parsley
10g fresh tarragon
15g fresh chives

Blitz all the ingredients together in a blender until smooth.

Caesar Dressing

This is the classic dressing for a Caesar salad. It can also be used as a dip for chicken wings, and even in sandwiches – try it with a tuna sarnie or a BLT.

MAKES ABOUT 360G

50g peeled garlic cloves
About 300g semi-skimmed milk
50g mature Cheddar, grated
35g drained anchovy fillets
25g egg yolk
15g Dijon mustard
1 tsp sherry vinegar
1 tsp lemon juice
85g olive oil
85g grapeseed oil
1 tsp truffle-infused olive oil

Put the garlic cloves into a pan and pour on enough milk to cover. Add a splash of cold **water** and slowly bring to a simmer. Drain the garlic and rinse under cold **water**. Repeat the process twice, using fresh milk and **water**. (This mellows the flavour of the garlic.) Leave to cool.

Put the cold, blanched garlic into a blender and add the cheese, anchovies, egg yolk, mustard, sherry vinegar and lemon juice. Blitz for 2 minutes, stopping after 1 minute to scrape down the sides of the jug to ensure even blitzing. With the motor running on a medium speed, slowly drizzle in the oils and blitz until they are fully incorporated and the dressing is completely emulsified.

Note: The egg yolk in this dish is raw. If you're wary of eating uncooked egg, use pasteurised egg yolks instead.

'Boiled' Dressing

This is a taste of history. Before the end of the 1800s, olive oil (or other salad oil) wasn't easy to come by unless you were lucky enough to live in southern Europe, so instead people used eggs and vinegar as the base for a creamy sauce known as a 'Boiled' dressing (which in truth is simmered rather than boiled). Turns out, our ancestors knew a thing or two, as this dressing is great for potato salads and equally delicious served over fish.

MAKES ABOUT 360G

145g **water**
18g plain flour
1 tbsp unrefined caster sugar
¼ tsp mustard powder
Pinch of salt
Pinch of sweet paprika
2 medium eggs
55g white wine vinegar
30g unsalted butter, diced
Splash of lemon juice (optional)
Fresh herbs, finely chopped, to taste (optional)

Pour the **water** into a bowl and add the flour, sugar, mustard powder, salt and sweet paprika. Whisk until well combined.

In a separate heatproof bowl, whisk the eggs and wine vinegar together then place the bowl over a pan of simmering **water** (bain-marie). Add the **water** mixture to the bowl and continue to whisk as the mixture slowly cooks, until it is thick and smooth.

Remove the bowl from the heat and gradually whisk in the butter. Taste the dressing at this stage. If it is too rich, add a splash of lemon juice.

Feel free to add finely chopped fresh herbs, to flavour the dressing. Chervil goes particularly well, but any soft, sweet herbs are good starting points: coriander, for example, or basil, tarragon or parsley. Just think about which herbs might best suit the dish you are dressing.

5

Culinary Excursions and Explorations

Where do you want to eat tonight?

Popcorn Popcorn Chicken

•

Tortilla and Three Tacos

Prawn Tacos with Pico de Gallo

Steak and Refried Beans Tacos

Vegetable and Guacamole Tacos

•

Moroccan Pasties

•

Ratatouille

•

Pasta Puttanesca

•

Curry Night

Chicken Tikka Kebab

Lamb Curry

Cauliflower and Chickpea Curry

Aubergine and Spinach Biryani

Naan

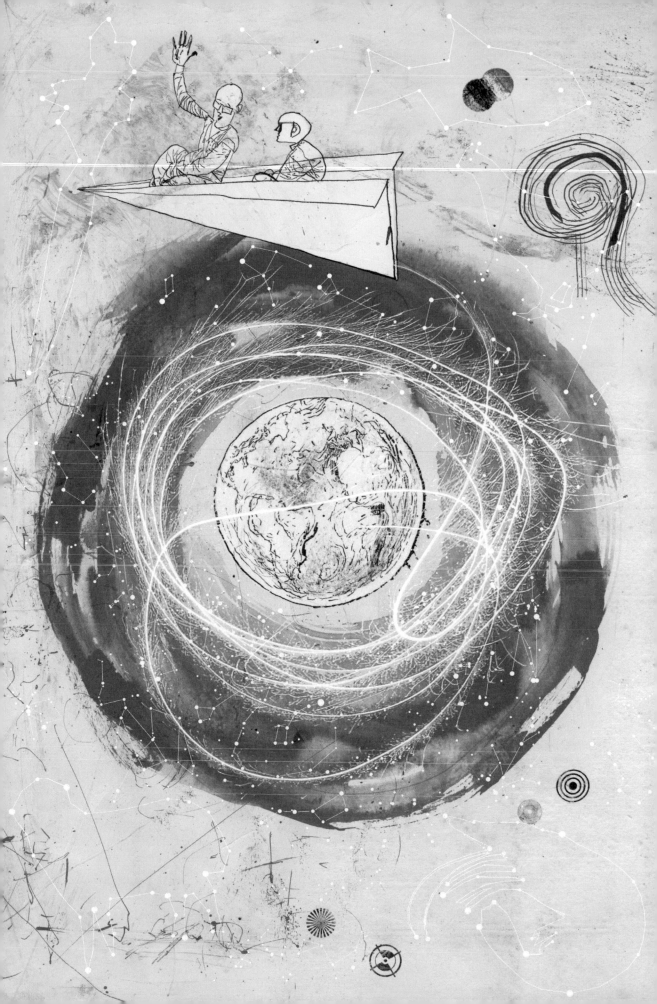

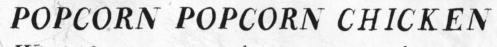

POPCORN POPCORN CHICKEN

What if you could make popcorn chicken with actual popcorn!?

What do you think of when you smell popcorn?
For me – and I suspect for many of you, too –
that aroma takes me to the movies.

This is surely one of the beauties of food and cooking:
the associations it evokes, the memories of past pleasures,
and the anticipation of other pleasures to come.
So, I began thinking about food and film and that
Saturday-night takeaway on the sofa – and that's when the
possibility of popcorn popcorn chicken popped into my head.
It's such a simple recipe it could be the perfect
accompaniment to a film.

So why not enjoy the sights, sounds, smell and feel of making
this dish as a prelude to settling down to whatever movie
magic floats your boat?
Or doesn't, if your favourite film is The Titanic,
The Poseidon Adventure or The Perfect Storm...

Popcorn Popcorn Chicken

For the marinated chicken
400g boneless, skinless chicken thighs
60g masa harina (Mexican nixtamalized cornflour)
240g kefir

For the popcorn chicken coating
40g puffed popcorn
130g masa harina (Mexican nixtamalized cornflour)
1 tbsp onion powder
4 tsp garlic powder
1½ tsp smoked paprika
2 tsp paprika
2 tsp salt
Black pepper

To cook
Vegetable oil, for deep-frying

Dice the chicken into 2–3cm pieces and place in a bowl. Put the masa harina flour into a separate bowl and stir in the kefir until smoothly combined. Pour this over the chicken and mix gently until evenly coated. Cover and leave to marinate in the fridge for at least 30 minutes.

For the coating, briefly blitz the puffed popcorn in a blender or food processor into smaller pieces. Tip into a bowl and combine with the remaining ingredients, including a very generous amount of freshly ground black pepper.

When ready to cook, heat the oil in a deep-fat fryer or other deep heavy-based pan (it should be no more than half-filled) to 160°C. Use a thermometer probe to check the temperature.

Remove the chicken pieces from the marinade. Working in batches, toss them in the popcorn mixture and set aside on a plate.

Deep-fry the coated chicken pieces in batches in the hot oil for 3–4 minutes until golden and cooked through, then remove and drain on kitchen paper.

Serve the popcorn popcorn chicken hot.

You could use baby sweetcorn instead of chicken – then you'd have corn inside corn inside corn. Or you could serve the baby sweetcorn with your popcorn chicken. Or try using king prawns or fish goujons instead of chicken.

For me this is an almost therapeutic experience for the senses. The pleasing, taco-like smell of the flour. The slop-slop-slop sound as you mix the chicken and kefir. It's one of those moments in the kitchen where you can go almost trance-like and enjoy the process, the doing.

Deep-fat frying, too, can have an almost meditative aspect to it. The soothing sound of the bubbling oil, like rain falling. If you listen in – get on the same frequency – you start to notice the sound changing as the coating crisps and the chicken cooks. Relaxing you into the movie to come, maybe, because it's soon ready, and you're ready to go.

This would be delicious dipped in a spicy mayonnaise, ketchup or even sweet chilli sauce.

TORTILLA AND THREE TACOS
How about getting street-food savvy?

The taco, a traditional Mexican dish consisting of tortilla with a filling, has become a key part of the street-food scene around the world. Which is not surprising since it offers versatility, variety and portability.

Over the following pages you'll find three delicious fillings: Prawns with pico de gallo; Steak with refried beans; and Vegetable and guacamole – but the possibilities are limited only by your imagination. In Mexico they like a taco with battered fish so you could team a tortilla with the recipe on page 210. Or you can have Chilli con carne (page 232) or pulled pork or ceviche, or whatever you can think up that might fit well in the folds of a flatbread.

You can, of course, buy tortillas, but making them is a lot of fun. You don't have to have a press to do it but, if kitchen kit is your thing, then this is a great excuse to go and buy one.

Tortillas

MAKES 12

250g masa harina (Mexican nixtamalized cornflour)
2g salt
250g **water**

To make the tortilla dough, put the masa harina and salt into an electric
mixer fitted with the paddle attachment. Pour in the **water** and mix on a
medium speed until a dough is formed, about 2 minutes. If you notice that the
mixture is not coming together as a dough, add a few 'flicks' of **water** until it does.
Cover with cling film and set aside to rest for 1 hour at room temperature.

Divide the dough into 12 even-sized pieces and shape into balls.
Roll each one between two sheets of baking paper until about 10–12cm
in diameter and 3mm thick.

To cook, heat a dry non-stick frying pan over a moderate heat. Cook the discs
of dough, one at a time, for 1 minute on each side until slightly charred.
Wrap in a clean tea towel to keep warm and soft while you cook the rest.

I'd hold back a bit of water at the start and add it if you need to. You're looking for a dough that's not tacky but a bit dry and almost crumbly.
You might think it's not going to roll well if it's like this, but it'll behave better than you expect.

It's better not to leave them lying around too long as they tend to dry out and become brittle and harder to work.

Prawn Tacos with Pico de Gallo

MAKES 12

36 raw king prawns

To marinate the prawns
Finely grated zest and juice of 1 lime
1 red chilli, finely chopped
4 sprigs of oregano, leaves picked
2 garlic cloves, peeled and finely grated
Pinch of ground cinnamon
½ tsp ground cumin
1 tbsp vegetable oil

For the Pico de gallo
½ white onion, peeled and finely diced
750g tomatoes
½ red chilli, finely chopped
Finely grated zest and juice of ½ lime
1 tbsp vegetable oil
Pinch of salt, to taste
Pinch of unrefined caster sugar, to taste

To assemble the tacos and serve
1 tbsp vegetable oil
Generous handful of fresh coriander (about 15g)
12 Tortillas (page 158)
½ Iceberg lettuce, thinly sliced
150g soured cream
2 avocados, halved, peeled, stoned and sliced
Chilli sauce (optional)
1 lime, cut into 4 wedges

For the marinade, combine all the ingredients in a large bowl. Add the prawns and turn to coat evenly. Cover and leave to marinate in the fridge for at least 2 hours.

For the Pico de gallo, soak the onion in cold **water** for 5 minutes to soften the raw flavour, then drain and place in a bowl. Quarter the tomatoes and scoop out the cores and seeds, leaving just thin petals; save the cores. Dice the fleshy petals then add to the onion with the chilli, and the lime zest and juice. Stir then set aside.

Heat the oil in a pan, add the reserved tomato cores and cook over a high heat, stirring, for about 1–2 minutes until broken down. Take off the heat and allow to cool. Strain through a fine-meshed sieve into the bowl of diced tomato and onion. Season with the salt and sugar. Discard the contents of the sieve.

To assemble, heat the oil in a pan, add the marinated prawns and cook over a medium heat, stirring regularly, for about 3 minutes until cooked through. Finely chop the coriander. Fill the tortillas with the prawns (3 in each), lettuce, chopped coriander, soured cream, sliced avocados and Pico de gallo, adding some chilli sauce if you like. Serve with lime wedges for squeezing.

Buying prawns with the shell on is a smart move because you get two things for the price of one – all those shells and heads are a flavour pack that can be used to make a shellfish stock, or used as the base for a seafood soup or ragu for pasta.

There is an easy way to prepare them.
Twist off the heads and peel the shell off starting at the head end. Pull away each shell segment as well as the tail. You will be left with only the fleshy body.

The digestive tract of each prawn needs to be removed.
Use a sharp paring knife to lightly slice along the back of the prawn to reveal the dark intestinal thread.
Pull it out and discard it.

Wash the prawns and pat dry before tipping into a bowl.

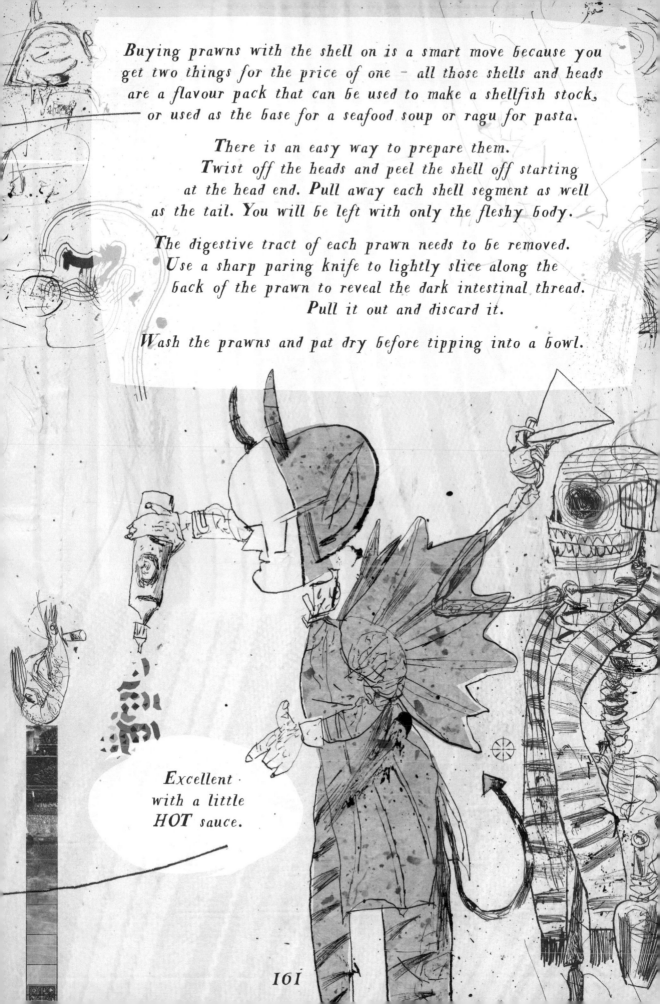

Excellent with a little HOT sauce.

Steak and Refried Beans Tacos

MAKES 4

2 freshly cooked steaks, rested (see page 206)

For the steak butter
125g unsalted butter, softened
2 tbsp olive oil
1½ tsp ground cumin
1 tsp chilli powder
1 tsp smoked paprika
1 tsp tomato ketchup
½ tsp Worcestershire sauce
Finely grated zest of 1 lime

For the refried beans
1 tbsp vegetable oil
2 garlic cloves, peeled and sliced
1 small red chilli, finely chopped
435g tin refried beans
40g beef stock
1 tsp chipotle paste (or Tabasco sauce)
Generous handful of fresh tarragon (6g)
Handful of fresh coriander (4g)
½ tsp lemon juice, or to taste
Salt and black pepper

To assemble the tacos
A little steak butter (from above)
4 Tortillas (page 158)
4 tbsp (heaped) Refried beans (from above)
Handful of shredded Iceberg lettuce
Small handful of Pickled red onion rings (page 164)
Small handful of fresh coriander leaves

For the steak butter, simply mix all the ingredients together in a bowl until evenly combined.

For the refried beans, heat the oil in a pan, add the garlic and chilli and fry until softened and golden. Tip into a bowl and add the refried beans, beef stock and chipotle paste. Finely chop the tarragon and coriander and stir through the mixture. Adjust the seasoning with the lemon juice, salt and freshly ground black pepper.

Return the steak strips to the pan the steaks were cooked in, add a little of the steak butter and warm through.

When you are ready to assemble the tacos, thinly slice the steaks.
Spread some of the refried bean mixture over each tortilla. Add the flavoured steak strips and cover with the shredded lettuce and pickled onion. Scatter the coriander over the tacos and serve.

This will combine most easily if the butter is softened, so it's worth removing it from the fridge several hours in advance.

It's incredibly easy to make and it's got plenty of umami from the ketchup and Worcestershire sauce, a kick from the chilli, zestiness from the citrus, smokiness from the paprika and spice from the cumin... everything you want from a street-food dish.

You'll have plenty of the delicious steak butter left over. Store it, well wrapped in the fridge, and use to pep up steaks, stir into chilli or melt over vegetables.

Vegetable and Guacamole Tacos

MAKES 4

For the pickled red onion
½ red onion, peeled and finely sliced into rings
40g red wine vinegar
Pinch of salt

For the guacamole
1 medium-large avocado
15g finely diced red chilli
15g peeled and finely diced red onion
2 tsp olive oil
Finely grated zest and juice of ½ lime
Pinch of smoked dried chilli flakes
Handful of fresh coriander
Salt and black pepper

For the vegetables
40g unsalted butter
5g peeled and grated fresh ginger
½ garlic clove, peeled and grated
Pinch of smoked dried chilli flakes
300g mixed broccoli florets and baby corn (or other veg of your choice)

To assemble the tacos and serve
4 Tortillas (page 158)
Handful of shredded Iceberg lettuce
Fresh coriander, to garnish

For the pickled red onion, simply combine all the ingredients in a small bowl and leave the onion to pickle for 30 minutes.

To make the guacamole, halve, peel and stone the avocado then roughly chop the flesh (you need 210g). Tip the chopped avocado into a bowl and mash, using the back of a fork. Add the chilli, onion, olive oil, lime zest and juice and the chilli flakes. Finely chop the coriander and stir into the mixture. Season with salt and freshly ground black pepper to taste. Cover and set aside until needed (but not for long).

For the vegetables, melt the butter in a pan along with the ginger, garlic and chilli flakes. Add the vegetables, cover and cook over a medium heat until the broccoli florets and baby corn are tender.

To assemble, divide the guacamole between the tortillas. Top with the cooked vegetables and shredded lettuce. Scatter over the pickled red onion rings, to taste. Finely chop the coriander and sprinkle over the tacos to serve.

With guacamole, you're looking to balance the creamy
richness of mashed avocado with something punchily
acidic (e.g. lime), something fragrant
(e.g. coriander), something a bit fiery (chilli)
and something textural (e.g. diced onion and diced chilli).
If there are other ingredients you like
in a guac - garlic or chopped tomato,
perhaps - then put them in.

Guacamole is best made not too far in
advance as it soon discolours when exposed to air.
You can protect it, however, by pressing
a piece of cling film onto the entire surface of the
guac and up the sides of the bowl, creating a seal
so that as little oxygen as possible can get at
the guacamole and turn it brown.

MOROCCAN PASTIES

When is a pasty not a pasty?

One of the fondest food memories from my childhood is of me and my sister sitting, wrapped in towels, in the open boot of my dad's old Cortina, after a stint on a windswept Cornish beach, eating Cornish pasties out of brown paper bags. It still sticks in my mind as one of life's great treats.

Messing about, then, with the pasty might seem an odd thing for me to do. And it's true that this culinary cultural crossover could at first appear surreal, almost comical – Bedouin meets Bodmin. But in fact, what is a pasty if not a pastry envelope into which you put a mixture of meat and veg? As such it offers huge scope for gastronomic creativity. I always find it really interesting to take a dish with a strong heritage or sense of place and play around with it. Shaking up conventions often helps us to see food in a new light, and maybe to change our relationship with it.

I've heard that the devil didn't enter Cornwall because he was frightened of the Cornishwoman's habit of putting anything and everything into a pasty, and thought he might be next. So, I'd say that, where pasties are concerned, there really are no rules.

Moroccan Pasties

MAKES 6

For the filling
1½ tsp cumin seeds
2 tbsp olive oil
400g diced beef, chopped into small pieces
1 onion, peeled and finely chopped
1 tbsp paprika
1 tbsp ground coriander
½ tbsp ground ginger
380g beef stock
2 cinnamon sticks
Salt and black pepper
Pinch of unrefined caster sugar (if needed)
120g peeled, finely diced potato (5mm dice)
2 tbsp pomegranate molasses
18 pitted green olives, halved
Handful of fresh coriander
Handful of fresh parsley

To assemble the pasties
3 large sheets ready-made shortcrust pastry
(all-butter, if possible), about 550g each
1 large egg, beaten
6 pinches of ground cinnamon
6 pinches of sesame seeds

For the sauce
80g tomato ketchup
80g harissa paste

For the filling, toast the cumin seeds in a dry, large non-stick pan over a medium-high heat until fragrant. Remove and set aside.

Heat the olive oil in the pan and, working in batches, fry the beef over a high heat until golden and caramelised on all sides. Remove the pieces using a slotted spoon and set aside in a bowl, leaving the oil in the pan. Reduce the heat to medium-low and add the onion (with a little more oil if needed). Cook until softened, then add the paprika, ground coriander and ginger. Cook until the pan starts to look dry.

Return the beef pieces and any resting juices to the pan and add the beef stock, toasted cumin seeds and cinnamon sticks. Bring to a simmer and reduce the heat to low. Cover the mixture with a cartouche and leave to cook until all the stock evaporates, and you are left with a thick, chunky mixture. This can take up to 1½ hours; you can remove the cartouche for the last 15–20 minutes.

Remove from the heat and season with salt and freshly ground black pepper, and a pinch of sugar if you think it is needed. Add the potato and set aside to cool a little, then stir in the pomegranate molasses.

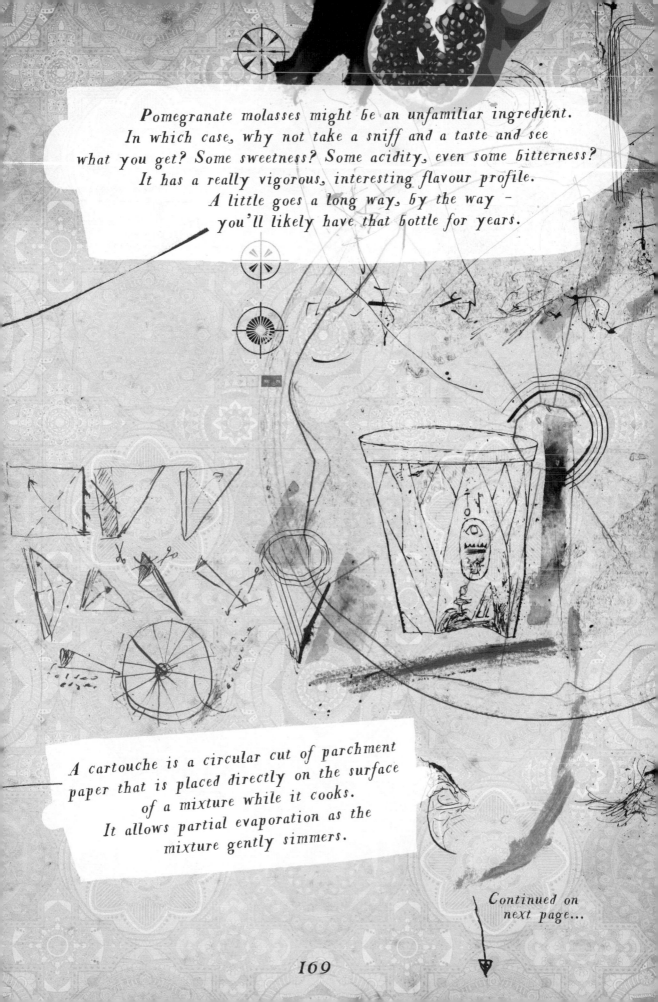

Pomegranate molasses might be an unfamiliar ingredient.
In which case, why not take a sniff and a taste and see
what you get? Some sweetness? Some acidity, even some bitterness?
It has a really vigorous, interesting flavour profile.
A little goes a long way, by the way –
you'll likely have that bottle for years.

A cartouche is a circular cut of parchment
paper that is placed directly on the surface
of a mixture while it cooks.
It allows partial evaporation as the
mixture gently simmers.

Continued on
next page...

169

Preheat the oven to 200°C/Fan 180°C/Gas 6 and lay a large silicone mat on a baking tray.

Unroll the 3 shortcrust pastry sheets and cut out 6 discs, about 17cm in diameter, using a plate or bowl as a guide.

Spoon the mixture onto the lower half of each pastry disc, leaving about a 2cm clear margin around the edge. Distribute the olive pieces evenly over the filling. Roughly chop the herbs and scatter those over the filling too.

Fold the top half of the pastry over to enclose the filling. Use your fingers to press the edges together to seal completely.

Place the parcels on the lined tray and lightly brush with the beaten egg. Scatter a pinch each of ground cinnamon and sesame seeds over each one. Bake in the oven for 35 minutes until golden.

In the meantime, to make the accompanying sauce, whisk the ketchup and harissa paste together in a bowl to combine.

Serve the pasties with the sauce on the side.

You could also make little folds along the edges
to make it prettier, if you want.
But the main thing is making sure it's
fully sealed so that it doesn't leak.

Another example of a culinary crossover,
this sauce is incredibly easy to do but makes
a perfect accompaniment for this pasty,
with the ketchup slightly dialling
down harissa's fieriness.
It's a condiment that can add a bit
of pep to all sorts of spicy meat dishes.

Towel,
old Cortina
and brown
paper bag
are optional.

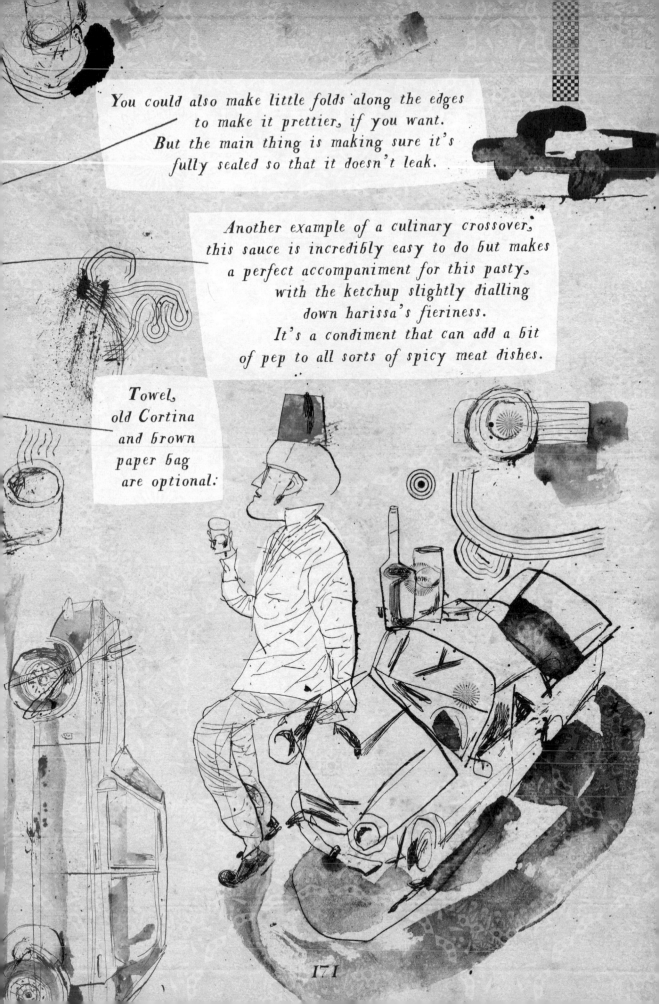

RATATOUILLE

Did you ever see the film Ratatouille?

Emotion, memories and associations play a big part
in how much we enjoy our food.
The film follows the fortunes of a rat who dreams of becoming a chef.
It's funny and fast-paced and probably the most accurate
gastronomic movie I've ever seen – which is not surprising
since my friend Thomas Keller was an adviser for the film.
However, the scene I love the most involves the grim-faced
food critic, Anton Ego (who, it is rumoured, was either
based on François Simon or on another friend of mine,
the late A.A.Gill).

When Ego tastes the rat's ratatouille, it's so flavoursome it
triggers big emotions and transports him right back to childhood.
I think of this as the 'Ratatouille Moment' and my goal is to make
all my dishes as evocative as this.

Ratatouille is probably the dish with which I have the greatest
emotional connection. Since I live in France, in season I can get hold
of all the necessary veg within a few hundred metres of my house.
It's an opportunity for a slow and languid cook, where you just
surrender to the flavours and aromas and the patient, dextrous
process of peeling and chopping and roasting and simmering
without worrying about the clock.

It'll be a half-day or so in the kitchen, maybe longer
(you could spread out the processes over a weekend, for example),
but there's the reward at the end of a totally delicious ratatouille
that's richly redolent of the Mediterranean.

Although to be honest, I'd say spending time in the kitchen doing
something like this is already incredibly rewarding.

Ratatouille

SERVES 4–6

For the tomato compote
2kg best-quality, ripe tomatoes (with stems), about 20–22
3 garlic cloves, peeled; 2 thinly sliced and 1 finely chopped
20–22 fresh basil leaves
Salt and black pepper
Generous pinch of unrefined caster sugar
2–4 sprigs of fresh thyme
2 sprigs of fresh tarragon
2 tbsp olive oil
1 onion, peeled and finely chopped
1 star anise
2 tsp tomato ketchup
Several drops of Worcestershire sauce
Bouquet garni (2 bunches of fresh thyme, 2 sprigs of fresh rosemary
and 2–4 sprigs of fresh tarragon, tied together)
Sherry vinegar, to taste
Maple syrup, to taste

For the ratatouille
1 small fennel bulb, coarse outer layer removed (about 130g trimmed weight)
2 aubergines, inner seed area removed (about 300g trimmed weight)
2 courgettes (about 450g trimmed weight)
Olive oil for cooking
1 quantity Tomato compote (from above)
2 peeled roasted red peppers (from a jar)
1 sprig of fresh thyme
1 sprig of fresh rosemary

To finish
Small handful of fresh tarragon
Handful of fresh basil
1 tsp coriander seeds
Tarragon vinegar, to taste

Tomato compote

To prepare the tomatoes, remove the stems and set aside for later. Using a small, sharp knife, gently prise out and discard the top core of each tomato. Also, make a very shallow criss-cross incision on the bottom of each one. Bring a large pan of **water** to the boil and have a large bowl of iced **water** to hand. You may need to work in batches, depending on the size of your pan. Add the tomatoes to the pan and blanch for 15 seconds. Immediately remove them, using a slotted spoon, and plunge into the iced **water** for 5 minutes.

Once all the tomatoes are done, peel away and discard the skins. Slice the tomatoes in half through the top, then use a teaspoon to scoop out all the flesh and seeds into a large sieve placed over a bowl. Set aside the hollowed-out tomato halves.

This compote takes some prepping
(get channelling your inner sous-chef)
and involves a lengthy roasting and stewing
of ingredients. Sometimes it does us good to
slow things down and take a different perspective.
A slow cook can produce a really
intense, complex depth of flavour.
You'll taste your own dedication and patience
right there on the plate.

Make a big batch of this compote and you've got
the key ingredient for other dishes too:
Tomato and coffee muffins (page 65),
Pasta puttanesca (page 179) and
Tomato compote ketchup (page 261).
Plus, you can use it to finish risottos,
spread it on toast, or embellish fish or sausages with it.

Continued on
next page...

Using the back of a wooden spoon, press the contents of the sieve through into the bowl underneath, extracting as much juice as possible. Discard the contents of the sieve. You should get approximately 500g tomato juice.

Divide the tomato halves into two equal batches. Roughly chop one batch into smaller pieces and add to the bowl of tomato juice.

Preheat the oven to 90°C/Fan 70°C/ lowest Gas and line a baking tray with baking paper.

Place the remaining tomato halves, cut side up, on the tray and put a sliver of garlic and a basil leaf on each one. Season with salt and freshly ground black pepper and sprinkle with the sugar. Top each with a snippet each of thyme and tarragon. Place in the low oven for about 3 hours, checking on the tomatoes every now and then. You want them softened, but still holding their shape (not as dry as store-bought sun-dried tomatoes).

Meanwhile, heat the olive oil in a large pan over a medium heat, add the onion, star anise and chopped garlic and cook gently until softened, without colour. Add the tomato ketchup and Worcestershire sauce and stir well to combine then add the chopped tomatoes and juice. Bring to a gentle simmer, reduce the heat to low and cook for 2½–3 hours, adding the bouquet garni halfway through cooking.

Once the tomatoes in the oven are done, remove and discard the garlic and herbs, then roughly chop the softened tomatoes and add them to the pan.

Cook the tomato compote for a further 1 hour or until the mixture is completely jammy. For the last 20 minutes, add the tomato stems that you set aside. When the compote is done, remove and discard the herbs, star anise and tomato stems. Taste and adjust the seasoning with a little sherry vinegar and maple syrup.

Ratatouille
Preheat the oven to 190°C/Fan170°C/Gas 5. Finely chop the fresh vegetables into 5mm dice, keeping them separate.

Heat a very generous glug of olive oil in a large pan and cook the vegetables separately until softened: allow 4–5 minutes for the fennel over a moderate heat; 3–4 minutes for the aubergines over a high heat; 2–3 minutes for the courgettes over a high heat. As each batch of vegetables is cooked, remove with a slotted spoon, leaving the oil in the pan.

Combine the cooked vegetables and tomato compote. Chop the roasted peppers and add them in. Season with salt and add the thyme and rosemary. Transfer to a large baking dish and cook in the oven for 10–15 minutes

Just before serving, pick out and discard the rosemary and thyme sprigs. Finely chop the tarragon and basil and stir through the ratatouille. Scatter over the coriander seeds and add a little tarragon vinegar if you like.

Once you've added the bouquet garni,
taste the mixture every **20** minutes or so.
If you find the flavour of the herbs
is becoming too strong, remove them as
we only want them to add 'warmth'.

When the compote is ready, it will have taken
on a wonderful deep red colour and become
almost jam-like. It will keep in the fridge, in
a covered container, for up to 5 days.

This might seem fiddly
(although there's a strange geometrical pleasure to be had in
achieving cuboid uniformity – or maybe that's just me),
but it means the veg cook evenly and at the same rate.
And by cutting them so small, the surface area is increased,
giving more flavour.

You want them softened but still with some 'bite' and,
ideally, you want to avoid getting any colour or
caramelisation on the vegetables, so keep an eye on them,
stirring regularly and taking the pan
on and off the heat as required.

PASTA PUTTANESCA

Have I really got time to make a compote that takes more than four hours?

The heart of the previous recipe, the thing that gives my ratatouille
its character and flavour profile, is the tomato compote,
which has a wonderful, concentrated, almost jam–like tomatoeyness.
I think it's incredible and I really want to convince you to have
a go at it. My strategy is to offer you a variety of recipes that
use it, so that if you make a large batch, you're rewarded with
a lot of options.

This is one of those options.
If you've got some compote in the fridge (it keeps really well),
then you've got the makings of a simple, quick pasta sauce
with a satisfyingly complex flavour.

Pasta Puttanesca

SERVES 1

1 portion of pasta of your choice
1 tbsp olive oil
1 garlic clove, peeled and finely chopped
½ red chilli, finely chopped
1 anchovy fillet, drained and finely chopped
130g Tomato compote (page 174)
4 pitted black olives, sliced or chopped
5g drained small lilliput capers (or roughly chopped larger capers)
5g finely grated Parmesan, plus extra to finish
Small handful of fresh tarragon (or parsley or chives if you prefer)
Splash of sherry vinegar
Salt and black pepper

Cook the pasta according to the packet instructions. Before draining, set aside 100g of the pasta cooking **water** for the sauce.

Heat the olive oil in a pan and add the garlic, chilli and anchovy. Cook, stirring regularly, over a moderate heat until the garlic softens and starts to turn golden.

Add the tomato compote along with the reserved cooking **water** and simmer for 5 minutes until most of the **water** has evaporated and the sauce has a loose, jammy consistency.

Stir in the olives, capers and grated Parmesan (which does a great job of thickening the sauce), then tip in the cooked, drained pasta. Chop the herbs and stir through the mixture, ensuring the pasta is coated well in the sauce.

Finish with a splash of sherry vinegar and some freshly ground black pepper. Serve scattered with a little more grated Parmesan.

Taste a little of the sauce at this stage –
do you think it needs more salt, or have
the anchovies, capers and olives
already seasoned it enough?

Have a taste of the sherry vinegar: what do you
think of it in comparison to other vinegars?
More savoury, maybe? More flavoursome? Nuttier?
It's a great thing to have on hand to add a little
acidity and complexity to a dish.
As you'll notice in this book,
I use it as a seasoning all the time.

CURRY NIGHT

I love Indian food.
It's probably one of the things I miss
most now that I live in France.
I was about ten when I visited my first curry
house and ordered a chicken korma -
the classic choice for a nervous first-timer -
and I've been a fan ever since.

It's not just the cuisine, I love the ritual
and the clichés that surround the
curry house experience and make it what it is:
the paisley wallpaper, the heating trays
the food is perched on, the music
(all sitar-drone, pipe-warble and tabla-thrum,
sometimes played at such a discreet volume you register
it subliminally rather than acoustically), the little
dented copper jugs the water is served in, the unfamiliar
beer brands you never drink anywhere else.

This, of course, is deeply nostalgic and shaped by my
memories from the 1970s, but whether or not your
experience is very different, we will still have a shared
belief in the excitement, emotion and pleasure of sitting
down to a spicy feast together with friends,
dipping into all the different dishes, having a laugh,
having a beer, communing over food.
In preparation for this book, my development team
came over to France and we cooked the selection of
dishes that follow.

It wasn't the typical curry house setting
- no tabla or sitar, just the insistent zizzizzizz
of the cicadas - but it was still absolute magic.
A moment of real human connectivity.
It's something we all need, and cooking
and eating can provide it.

Chicken Tikka Kebab

SERVES 4-6

10 chicken thighs, skinned and boned

For the marinade
400g extra-thick (or hung) yoghurt
20g peeled, roughly chopped garlic cloves
4 tsp garam masala
10g Kashmiri chilli powder
¼ tsp smoked paprika
¾ tsp ginger powder
2¾ tsp salt

To serve
Lemon wedges
Raitziki, optional (page 255)

Put the skinned, boneless chicken thighs into a large bowl.

Place all the ingredients for the marinade in a blender or food processor and blitz until smooth. Pour the mixture over the chicken and combine well, ensuring the chicken is evenly coated. Cover and place in the fridge to marinate overnight.

When you're ready to cook, preheat the oven grill to maximum or heat up your barbecue.

If oven-cooking, spread the chicken thighs out on a foil-lined tray and grill until cooked through, about 25–30 minutes. Alternatively, you could thread the chicken onto skewers and cook them on the barbecue, turning regularly, until tender and cooked through. To check, insert a small knife into the thickest part: the flesh should no longer be pink.

Pile the chicken onto a warm plate and serve with lemon wedges and a bowl of Raitziki, if you like.

Blend, marinate, grill – this has got to be one of the easiest recipes to rustle up, with a depth of flavour that belies its simplicity.

You want the thickest yoghurt you can get your hands on, as this will coat the chicken most effectively. Too thin and it'll slide off so you won't get that grilled melding of meat and marinade. If you can't get hold of any, or you just want to try out a new technique, you can thicken your own: see page 259.

One of the best bits, for me, is when the yoghurty spicy marinade blackens in places, introducing a lovely char to the mix of flavours.

The chicken should reach an internal temperature of 68°C; this is best checked using a probe thermometer.

Lamb Curry

SERVES 4–6

1kg trimmed boneless lamb leg, cut into 3cm pieces (sinew removed)

For the marinade
350g extra-thick (or hung) yoghurt (to thicken your own, see page 259)
2 tsp salt
½ tsp chilli powder
½ tsp asafoetida powder
¾ tsp ground coriander

For the base
100g vegetable oil or ghee
2 black cardamom pods
½ cinnamon stick
250g peeled and finely diced onion (about 2 medium)
60g peeled and finely grated garlic (about 16–18 cloves)
20g peeled and finely grated fresh ginger
1 tsp ground turmeric
2 tsp chilli powder
2 tsp garam masala
200g passata
About 150g **water**

To finish
Handful of fresh coriander

For the marinade, combine the ingredients in a large bowl. Tip in the lamb and combine well until the pieces are evenly coated. Cover, then place in the fridge to marinate for at least 2 hours or, even better, overnight.

For the base, heat the oil or ghee in a large pan over a moderate heat. Add the cardamom and cinnamon and let their flavours infuse the oil until it becomes aromatic.

Add the diced onion and cook until softened. Toss in the garlic and ginger and continue to cook until the mixture becomes dry and starts smelling sweet; this can take up to 5 minutes.

Add the turmeric, chilli powder and garam masala and cook for 1–2 minutes. Tip in the passata and cook until the mixture is reduced and thickens and most of the liquid has evaporated, about 10 minutes.

Add the marinated meat and leave to simmer for 5 minutes until the lamb begins to cook. You will notice how the fat leaches out of the yoghurt, which is the point at which it could burn, so add enough **water** to cover the meat and leave to simmer, uncovered, for 1½–2 hours until the meat is tender and the sauce has mellowed and become really rich.

Serve the lamb curry garnished with fresh coriander.

On a curry night,
I'd want a lamb dish like this,
enriched with the deep, complex,
vibrant spiciness that comes from
a long, slow simmer.

Asafoetida is a key spice in this recipe.
The name means 'stinking resin'
(it is in fact the resin of
giant fennels), so you know already it's
going to be seriously smelly, but take
a sniff or two. You may find it
somewhat unpleasant but just wait
and see what happens as it cooks
and calms down, adding a meaty
oniony depth to the dish.

This bit of the cook is just a series of spicy
sensory moments to be enjoyed.
First, floral citrussy cardamom
and woody cinnamon...

...then lemony woodiness
and a punch of sulphurousness...

...warm, nutty turmeric and possibly
some floral, resinous, pine and even
balsamic notes from the garam masala;
a fruity kick from the chilli...

Cauliflower and Chickpea Curry

SERVES 4–6

2 tbsp ghee or vegetable oil
3 medium onions, peeled and sliced
8 garlic cloves, peeled and sliced
1 tsp salt
1 medium cauliflower (about 450g)
4 tbsp Rogan Josh (or Madras) paste
2 tbsp concentrated tomato purée
400g tin chickpeas

To finish
200g baby spinach
20g fresh coriander

Heat the ghee or oil in a large pan and add the onions, garlic and salt. Cook over a moderate heat until softened, about 5 minutes.

In the meantime, slice off the base of the cauliflower then cut into even-sized florets, saving the core and any trimmings (cut these into even-sized pieces). Set the florets aside for later.

Add the cauliflower trimmings to the onions and garlic and continue to cook for 10 minutes until the mixture softens and starts to look dry.
Add the curry paste and tomato purée and cook for a further 5 minutes, stirring regularly.

Tip the chickpeas into the pan, along with the liquid from the can, then fill the can with **water** and add this too. Bring the mixture to a simmer and simmer for 5–10 minutes.

Remove the pan from the heat and tip the mixture into a blender. Blitz to a very smooth sauce.

In the meantime, blanch the cauliflower florets in a pan of boiling **water** for about 4 minutes until tender. Drain well.

Return the sauce to the pan, tip in the cooked cauliflower florets and season with salt to taste. Stir in the spinach and allow it to wilt into the mixture.
Finely chop the coriander and scatter over the curry just before serving.

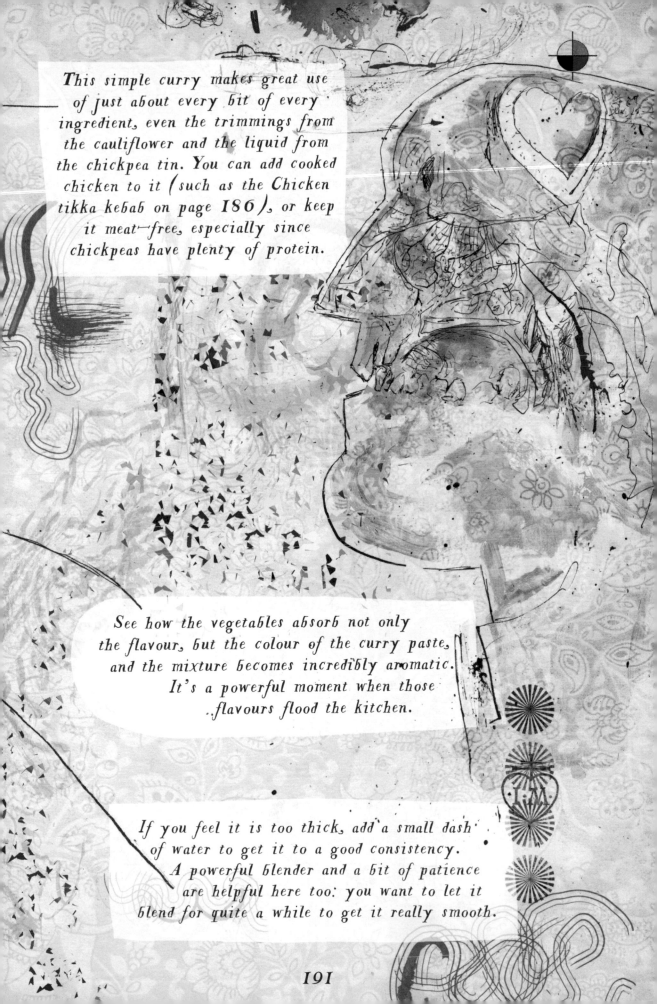

This simple curry makes great use of just about every bit of every ingredient, even the trimmings from the cauliflower and the liquid from the chickpea tin. You can add cooked chicken to it (such as the Chicken tikka kebab on page 186), or keep it meat-free, especially since chickpeas have plenty of protein.

See how the vegetables absorb not only the flavour, but the colour of the curry paste, and the mixture becomes incredibly aromatic. It's a powerful moment when those ..flavours flood the kitchen.

If you feel it is too thick, add a small dash of water to get it to a good consistency. A powerful blender and a bit of patience are helpful here too: you want to let it blend for quite a while to get it really smooth.

Aubergine and Spinach Biryani

SERVES 2–4

For the onion mix
100g ghee
750g peeled and finely chopped onions (about 6–7)
20g peeled and finely chopped garlic

For the Madras aubergine
600g finely chopped aubergine flesh (about 2–3)
15g Madras curry powder
Salt
Ghee for cooking
2 tsp coriander seeds

For the spinach and yoghurt mix
2 tsp nigella seeds
1½ tsp garam masala
2 tsp cumin seeds
2½ tsp ground coriander
1½ tsp ground allspice
½ tsp ground turmeric
10g Madras curry powder
Pinch of chilli powder
Black pepper
200g baby spinach leaves
300g Greek yoghurt

For the fragrant rice
50g raisins
40g flaked almonds
120g basmati rice
2 tsp fennel seeds
9 green cardamom pods
6 black cardamom pods
6 whole cloves
3 bay leaves (fresh or dried)
1 litre **water**

To assemble and cook
5 green cardamom pods
5 cloves
1 sheet ready-made puff pastry (all-butter, if possible)
1 large egg, whisked with a pinch of salt (egg wash)
Handful of fennel seeds and cumin seeds (or 2 handfuls of store-bought Bombay mix)

To serve
Handful of fresh coriander
Raitziki, optional (page 255)

ARE YOU READY FOR AN AROMA EXPLOSION?

Traditionally, one of the main goals with this dish is making sure the cooking vessel is tightly sealed so that the rice ends up lovely and fluffy.

You could, of course, just trust a close-fitting lid. Some recipes suggest further sealing the lid with foil or a strip of pastry but, if you've gone that far, why not make the pastry part of the dish?

And why not trap as much aroma as possible under that pastry lid?

Then you have the visual pleasure of a shiny brown crust and the textural pleasure of something crispy being part of the meal.

But beyond all that, there'll be that wonderful moment when you tap through the crust, hear the crunch of the pastry breaking apart, and then smell all the spectacular spicy smells escaping from it.

Continued on next page...

To prepare the onion mix, melt the ghee in a large pan over a medium heat. Add the onions and garlic and cook until softened and golden, about 10–15 minutes. Remove from the heat and set aside.

For the Madras aubergine, put the diced aubergine into a large bowl, sprinkle over the Madras powder and season with salt. Mix well to coat the diced aubergine evenly. You will need to cook the aubergine in 2 or 3 batches. In your largest pan, heat a generous amount of ghee over a medium heat. Add a batch of aubergine and cook until softened and golden. Remove to a tray lined with kitchen paper. Repeat to cook the rest. Tip all the aubergine into a large bowl, add half the cooked onion mixture along with the coriander seeds and mix well to combine. This will make your Madras aubergine layer.

To prepare the spinach and yoghurt mix, put all the spices into a large dry pan over a medium heat, adding a generous crack of freshly ground black pepper. Fry lightly for a minute until the spices release their aromas then tip in all the spinach. Cook until the spinach wilts completely, then add the remaining cooked onion mixture and take the pan off the heat. Stir in the yoghurt and season with a little salt. This will make your spinach and yoghurt layer.

For the fragrant rice, soak the raisins in enough hot **water** to cover for 30 minutes, then drain and set aside. Toast the flaked almonds in a dry pan over a medium-high heat until golden; remove to a plate and set aside. Rinse the rice under cold, running **water** to remove excess starch.

In a large, dry pan, toast the fennel seeds, cardamom pods and cloves for 2 minutes until fragrant. Add the bay leaves, pour in the **water** and season with salt. Bring to the boil and add the rice. Cover and simmer for 10–12 minutes until cooked. Drain well, then add the toasted almonds and raisins and stir though the rice. Set aside.

To assemble, start by toasting the cardamom pods and cloves in a hot, dry pan until fragrant. Remove to a plate and set aside for now. Have ready a suitable baking dish, about 20 x 13cm and 10cm deep.

Spoon the Madras aubergine into the baking dish and spread out evenly. Cover with the spinach and yoghurt mixture. On top of this, spread out the fragrant rice. Ensure all the layers are even, and spread right into the corners. Scatter over the toasted cardamom and cloves.

Lay the sheet of puff pastry on top of the dish, allowing the excess to hang over the sides. Pinch the edges to seal to the rim of the dish and brush the egg wash generously over the pastry. Place in the fridge to rest for 20 minutes while you preheat the oven to 230°C/Fan 220°C/Gas 8.

Trim away any excess pastry then place the dish in the oven and bake for 10 minutes. Turn the oven down to 200°C/Fan 180°C/Gas 6 and take the dish from the oven. Brush the pastry with a little more egg wash and sprinkle fennel and cumin seeds (or Bombay mix) on top. Bake for a further 15–20 minutes.

Carefully remove the dish from the oven. Using a sharp knife, cut into portions to serve and scatter over more seeds (or Bombay mix) for extra crunch and a big boost of spicy flavour. Chop the coriander and scatter this over too. Delicious served with Raitziki.

You want every cube of aubergine to be in contact with the base of the pan as that's how they'll take on colour, so don't overcrowd it.

This helps prevent your rice becoming too sticky and clumping together.

Ideally, you want an air gap between the pastry and the underlying layers. It'll help the pastry stay crispy and act as a holding tank for all those spicy aromas.

The first high-heat bake ensures that the pastry holds shape and forms a crust.

For me, this is probably the best moment of the whole cook. Get your knife ready to crack that crust and release the aromas!

(By the way, if you spot any of the whole spices that were added – cardamom and cloves – remove them, as they're not so nice to bite down on.)

195

Naan

MAKES 8

2 tsp active dried yeast (7g)
Pinch of unrefined caster sugar
1½ tbsp warm **water**
450g strong white bread flour
140g whole milk
150g Greek yoghurt
1 large egg
2 tsp salt
½ tsp nigella seeds

For the garlic ghee
65g ghee
10g peeled and finely chopped garlic (about 3 large cloves)

Combine the yeast, sugar and warm water in a small bowl and set aside at room temperature for 5–10 minutes to activate the yeast.

Put the flour, milk, yoghurt and egg into a stand mixer fitted with the dough hook attachment. Add the activated yeast to the bowl and mix on low speed until the mixture comes together as a dough. Cover the bowl with cling film and set aside to rest for 10 minutes.

Now add the salt to the dough and continue to mix on medium speed for about 10 minutes until it becomes elastic.

Divide the dough into 8 even-sized pieces, about 100g each, and shape into balls. Place on a lightly oiled tray and cover loosely with lightly oiled cling film. Leave to rise at room temperature for 2–3 hours until doubled in size.

In the meantime, prepare the garlic ghee. Melt the ghee in a small pan over a low heat, add the garlic then take off the heat and leave to infuse.

Once the dough has proved, pick up a dough ball with one hand and use your other hand to form it into a teardrop shape, about 7mm thick. Repeat the process with the remaining balls of dough. Sprinkle the nigella seeds over the surface of the dough and gently press them in.

Preheat the oven to its highest setting and place a pizza stone on the top shelf. Once the oven is up to temperature and the pizza stone is hot, lay a piece of dough on the stone, seeds side up, and cook for 2–2½ minutes. Set aside on a wire rack and repeat to cook the remaining pieces of dough.

Once all the naan are cooked, turn the oven to a low setting and return all the naan to the oven for a few minutes to warm through. Meanwhile, gently reheat the garlic ghee. To serve, brush the naan with the warm garlic ghee.

Ghee is a form of clarified butter.
Clarified butter has been heated to remove
whey and milk solids so that it can be heated
to a higher temperature without burning.
Ghee takes this one step further, cooking until the milk
solids go brown, which gives it a particular flavour.
You can make this yourself or it's readily
available in supermarkets and Asian stores.

You will notice how the
mixture starts to bubble,
which is the yeast converting
the sugar to carbon dioxide.
And it's the carbon dioxide that
is going to aerate our dough
and make it pillowy.

This resting process is
known as 'autolyse':
it allows the flour to soak up
the liquid before the gluten is
developed by kneading
the dough.

Adding the salt earlier would
hinder the autolyse process.

The dough should have a smooth
consistency and bounce back
when you press on it.
It will also no longer be sticky.

If you wet your hands
a little, it should help
prevent sticking.

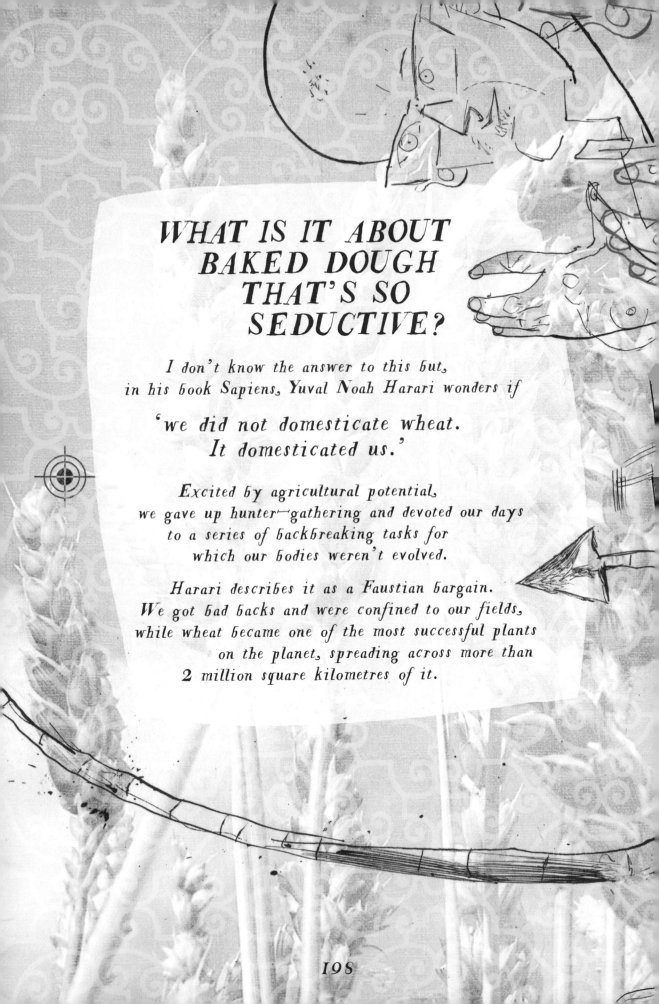

WHAT IS IT ABOUT BAKED DOUGH THAT'S SO SEDUCTIVE?

I don't know the answer to this but,
in his book Sapiens, Yuval Noah Harari wonders if

'we did not domesticate wheat.
It domesticated us.'

Excited by agricultural potential,
we gave up hunter-gathering and devoted our days
to a series of backbreaking tasks for
which our bodies weren't evolved.

Harari describes it as a Faustian bargain.
We got bad backs and were confined to our fields,
while wheat became one of the most successful plants
on the planet, spreading across more than
2 million square kilometres of it.

So maybe it's part of wheat's cunning plan,
  but I love naan. And, while elsewhere in this book
I've tried to encourage a relaxed approach to cooking,
  there's something about this bread that presses my
precision button. As far as I'm concerned, it has to be
served straight away.

Out of the oven, there's a moment, after around a couple
of minutes, when the bread starts to relax.
    When it's at its softest and steamiest but still fresh.
When it's still slightly inflating and everything
    is in equilibrium.

        That's when I want to eat it.
        Any later and it starts to deflate,
        at which point, for me,
        the experience of eating it can become
        a little deflating as well.

        To paraphrase an old saying,
            'Time waits for no naan.'

6

Traditional Deliciousness

*Why don't we all get together over
a classic?*

Steak with Pan Jus

•

Fish and Chips

•

Spaghetti Carbonara

•

Fish Cakes with Tartare Sauce

•

Mac 'n' Cheese

•

Chilli Con Carne with Spiced Chocolate

•

Roast Potatoes, Roast Chicken and Gravy,
Yorkshire Puddings

Let's put the ritual back into the habitual.

A decade or so ago, a friend of a friend of mine lost his sense of smell, a condition known as 'anosmia'. This means that, while he can still experience the five tastes — salt, sugar, sour, bitter, umami — which are detected in the mouth, he can't experience the trillion or so aromas that are detected in the nose. Since flavour is a combination of taste and aroma, he lives in a world without flavour.

Dan is eloquent about his situation. He talks about how thinned-down, monochromatic and one-dimensional a flavourless world is. And he points out just how social food is. So much of what we do for fun and relaxation centres on eating and drinking, whether it's a trip to the pub, popcorn at the cinema, a restaurant outing, a movie and a takeaway, or a meal round a table with family or friends.

We need to feed ourselves on a regular basis, so it's perhaps inevitable that it becomes habitual rather than a ritual. It's easy for us to forget how transformative and stimulating cooking and eating can be. How much it nourishes, in all senses — not just feeding the belly, feeding the soul.

A classic dish can stir the emotions, trigger excitement and anticipation, and give us a bit of magic. A memory to treasure. A moment that gives life 'meaning'.

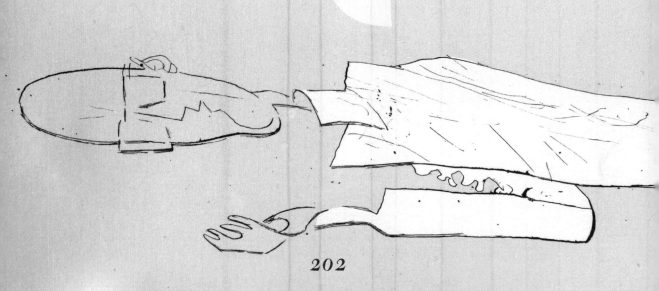

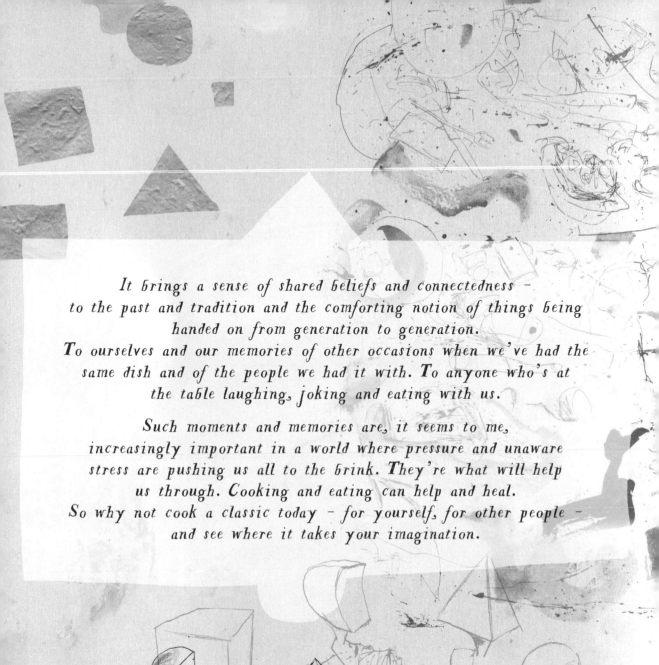

It brings a sense of shared beliefs and connectedness –
to the past and tradition and the comforting notion of things being
handed on from generation to generation.
To ourselves and our memories of other occasions when we've had the
same dish and of the people we had it with. To anyone who's at
the table laughing, joking and eating with us.

Such moments and memories are, it seems to me,
increasingly important in a world where pressure and unaware
stress are pushing us all to the brink. They're what will help
us through. Cooking and eating can help and heal.
So why not cook a classic today – for yourself, for other people –
and see where it takes your imagination.

STEAK WITH PAN JUS

Time for a meat treat?

Some of the classics on the following pages you might serve up to dozens of people. That's probably less likely with a steak, not least because it's an expensive cut. More probably it's going to be a treat – possibly even just for yourself, a moment of culinary indulgence with a sense of occasion. Reward is, I'd say, an integral part of eating: if you take time and trouble to choose your ingredients, and then spend more time and energy preparing them, then that sense of effort and achievement enhances your enjoyment of what you eat. Picking out and paying for a beautiful rib-eye, criss-crossed with marbling, and then skilfully executing the technique to bring the best out of that cut, will confer a real sense of satisfaction – for the soul as well as the stomach.

Steak with Pan Jus

SERVES 1

1 rib-eye steak (about 220g)
Salt
A little vegetable oil
1 banana shallot (or small onion), peeled and finely sliced
2 tbsp **water**
10g unsalted butter
Sea salt flakes and black pepper

Remove the steak from the fridge about 30 minutes before cooking to bring it to room temperature. Season all over with salt and rub with a little oil.

Heat a heavy-based frying pan over a high heat. Once the pan is smoking, add the steak and cook, flipping it every 20 seconds. Continue doing this for about 2 minutes, then start checking the internal temperature of the steak using a probe thermometer. For a medium steak you're looking for the meat to ultimately reach 56°C, so when the probe reads 52°C, remove it from the pan.

Place the steak on a wire rack set over a tray and leave to rest for 5 minutes.

In the meantime, reduce the heat under the pan to medium-low and add 1 tsp oil. Now add the sliced shallot to the pan with a pinch of salt and cook until softened, stirring well and scraping up any bits of meat that have stuck to the bottom of the pan.

When the shallot is soft and starting to caramelise, add the **water**. Once simmering, add the butter and mix well to combine. Allow to reduce to about 1 tbsp sauce. Remove from the heat and season with salt and freshly ground black pepper.

Return the steak to the frying pan and spoon the sauce over the meat as it gently warms up.

Serve the steak topped with the saucy shallots and seasoned with sea salt flakes and freshly ground black pepper.

Searing – frying quickly over a high heat – is a great way to maximise the flavour from a piece of meat. The technical process happening during searing is the Maillard reaction. It takes place at around 120°C, so you need the pan to be hot. If you're cooking several steaks, you want to make sure you don't overcrowd the pan which will cool it down too much. In this circumstance, it's probably best to cook the meat in batches or more than one pan.

You're probably wondering what the flip's going on with all this flipping, and whether you can just cook the steak on one side then the other, in traditional fashion. And of course, you can. But this exposes the meat to a high heat for a long time, which means it might overcook. Frequent flipping gets round this because it allows the flesh to cool slightly before being subject to another blast of heat. It enables the meat to cook more evenly and gain a good crust. It's a versatile technique that you can apply to lamb chops and burgers as well.

It's tempting to skip this step, since that succulent slab of meat is calling, but I'd encourage you to resist if you can. There's still plenty of heat in the meat when you take it out of the pan. Resting it for 5 minutes or so allows that residual heat to finish cooking the flesh gently. Resting also lets the meat fibres relax so that they hold onto their juices, which means you get moister flesh.

FISH AND CHIPS

Do you want salt and vinegar on it?

It's our national dish and one of the few dishes in this country that everyone has an opinion about, from the type of fish – cod? haddock? plaice? whiting? – to whether the chips should be thick or thin. It's powerfully evocative too, from memories of takeaways (the jar of pickled eggs on the counter, the enticing stacks of crispy fish in the glass-fronted warmers, those funny little fish-shaped wooden forks) to memories of eating F & C by the seaside, wrapped in newspaper or piled on one of those polystyrene trays, with the smell of the sea in your nostrils and gulls trying to snatch a chip when you aren't looking. We all have a history with this dish, and an emotional connection. It's a real nostalgia trip, each time you eat it.

So I like to max out on the memories, by adding a seaweed salt to summon up that maritime tang of eating beside the seaside. And a chippy dip, inspired by those soggy bits of vinegary, squishy, mushy chip you find at the bottom of a bag o' chips.

As for the chips themselves, your average chippie probably doesn't triple-cook them, but long ago (before even the opening of *The Fat Duck*), I became obsessed with creating what for me was the perfect chip: crunchy on the outside and fluffy within. Eventually I worked out how to get what I wanted. It was the first dish that I invented, and it's since become popular around the globe. So I guess you could say it's become a classic too.

Fish and Chips

4 white fish fillets, such as cod, pollack,
coley, plaice, or even sole

For the seaweed salt
5 nori seaweed sheets
15g salt
10g kombu powder

For the pickled fennel seeds
40g white wine vinegar
1 tsp unrefined caster sugar
1 tsp salt
20g fennel seeds

For the bicarbonate batter
350g cold soda water
200g plain flour
1 tsp bicarbonate of soda
1 tsp unrefined caster sugar

To assemble and cook
Vegetable oil, for deep-frying
100g plain flour

To serve
Triple cooked chips and chippy dip (page 212)
Malt vinegar, to taste

For the seaweed salt, tear the nori into smaller pieces and place in a blender with the salt and kombu powder. Blitz well then transfer to an airtight container and set aside until needed.

For the pickled fennel seeds, heat the wine vinegar in a small pan, add the sugar and salt and stir until dissolved. Remove this pickling liquor from the heat and leave to cool. In the meantime, toast the fennel seeds in a hot dry pan for about 2 minutes until fragrant. Add the toasted seeds to the cooled pickling liquid, cover and store in the fridge (they will keep for several months). Drain before using.

For the batter, simply whisk all the ingredients together in a bowl. Set aside.

When ready to cook the fish, heat the oil in a deep-fat fryer, or other large, deep, heavy-based pan (it should be no more than half-filled) to 180°C.

Lightly dust the fish fillets in the flour, then drag each piece back and forth in the bowl of batter. Drop gently into the hot oil and fry until golden, turning the fish halfway through.

Remove the fish with a slotted spoon and place on a tray lined with kitchen paper to drain. Season with the seaweed salt and the pickled fennel seeds.
Serve at once, with your chips and dip, and vinegar if you like.

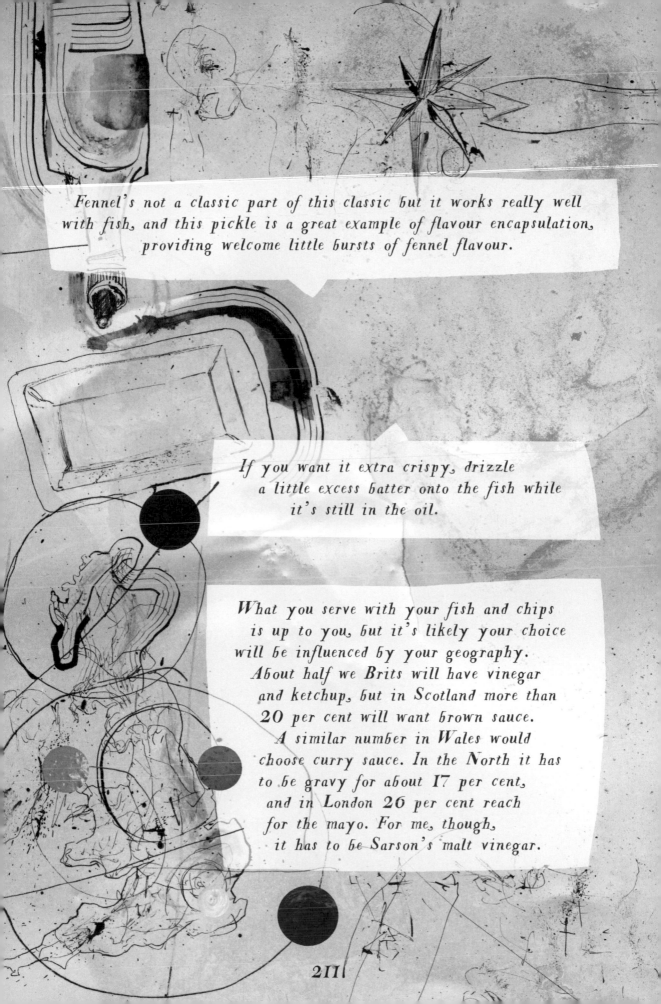

Fennel's not a classic part of this classic but it works really well with fish, and this pickle is a great example of flavour encapsulation, providing welcome little bursts of fennel flavour.

If you want it extra crispy, drizzle a little excess batter onto the fish while it's still in the oil.

What you serve with your fish and chips is up to you, but it's likely your choice will be influenced by your geography. About half we Brits will have vinegar and ketchup, but in Scotland more than 20 per cent will want brown sauce. A similar number in Wales would choose curry sauce. In the North it has to be gravy for about 17 per cent, and in London 26 per cent reach for the mayo. For me, though, it has to be Sarson's malt vinegar.

Triple Cooked Chips and Chippy Dip

SERVES 4

1kg Maris Piper potatoes
100g unsalted butter
2 tsp malt vinegar
Salt
Vegetable oil, for deep-frying
Sea salt flakes

Peel the potatoes and cut into chips, about 1.5cm thick and 6cm long. Reserve about 250g of the potato trimmings and offcuts, dicing them into smaller pieces.

Put the chips and diced trimmings into a large bowl and rinse under cold running **water** until the **water** runs clear.

Fill a large pan with about 2.5 litres cold **water** and add the chips and trimmings. Bring to the boil, then reduce the heat to a simmer and cook until the chips are almost falling apart. Gently remove the chips with a slotted spoon and lay them on a wire rack set over a tray to cool completely (preferably in the fridge).

Transfer the cooked trimmings to a bowl. While still warm, mash them with the butter, vinegar and a good pinch of salt. Taste to check the seasoning and then set aside; keep warm. This will be your dip.

Heat the oil in a deep-fat fryer, or other large, deep, heavy-based pan (it must be no more than half-filled) to 130°C. Fry the chips in small batches for about 5 minutes until a light crust forms, then remove and drain on a tray lined with kitchen paper. Lay the potatoes once again on a wire rack and leave to cool completely (preferably in the fridge).

To finish the chips, heat the oil in the pan to 180°C and fry the chips until golden, about 7 minutes. Drain on a tray lined with kitchen paper and scatter with sea salt flakes before serving, with the warm dip alongside.

This washes away excess starch, which would otherwise leach into the cooking water, rendering it gloopy.

This will take about 20-30 minutes, depending on the potato, and you'll need to be vigilant towards the end because the stage after 'close to falling apart' is... fallen apart.

Take a taste at this stage. Is the level of vinegar to your liking or do you want more?

You can store the chips at this stage in the fridge for up to 3 days.

SPAGHETTI CARBONARA
What shall I serve my unexpected guests?

Although it's a cliché to say Italians are passionate about their food, like a lot of clichés it happens to be true. I've been on many food fact-finding trips to Italy and I've yet to encounter anyone there who didn't have strong opinions on all matters culinary. For them, cuisine and conviviality go hand in hand, which is probably why they have a whole range of simple but delicious dishes that can be rustled up in minutes, should a gang of hungry people turn up.

Carbonara is one of these – a dish made with stuff you're likely to have in your fridge and larder that you can have on the table in the time it takes to cook the spaghetti.
A real communal crowd-pleaser.

Spaghetti Carbonara

20g salt
200g fresh or dried spaghetti
100g pancetta lardons
30g finely grated Parmesan
2 egg yolks
Black pepper

Pour 2 litres **water** into a large pan, add the salt and bring to the boil.
Once the **water** is boiling steadily, add the spaghetti and cook until *al dente*
(tender but with a bit of bite).

In the meantime, cook the pancetta lardons in a second large, deep pan
over a medium heat for about 5 minutes until crispy.

In a small bowl, combine the grated Parmesan and egg yolks and set aside.
A few minutes before the spaghetti will be done, add a small ladleful
(about 40g) of the cooking **water** to the egg mix, whisking well to combine.

Once the spaghetti is cooked, drain it well (reserving a little cooking **water** in case
you need it) and tip it into the pan of cooked pancetta lardons. Pour in the egg mix
and toss the mixture well to evenly coat all the spaghetti in the thick 'custard-like'
sauce. If it seems too thick, let it down with a little of the reserved cooking **water**.

Season with freshly ground black pepper and leave to sit for 2 minutes
before serving.

'I sometimes do a fairly robust version in which I start
by cooking a finely chopped onion and a puréed garlic
clove gently and slowly for about 15 minutes until softened
before adding the lardons and ½ chilli, chopped, and letting
everything take on some colour. After which I'd proceed
pretty much as above, and serve sprinkled with chopped
parsley.'

I've used just yolks to bring richness and an intensity of egg flavour. You could use whole eggs instead to see if you prefer a looser and less intense version.

There's no need for oil in the pan as the lardons will cook in their own fat. (If you don't have lardons, you could try chopped unsmoked streaky bacon – it won't have the same flavour and texture impact but you'll get a similar effect.)

This is where a magical metamorphosis happens, as the warmth of the pan, pasta and lardons contrives to convert the eggs into a silky sauce. There should be enough residual heat there so that you don't no need to return the pan to the heat. But if the mixture seems too cold and the eggs aren't thickening you could put it back on a gentle heat for a moment or two. (Any longer and you'll be edging towards overcooking it and may end up with a strange hybrid of pasta and scrambled eggs.)

FISH CAKES WITH TARTARE SAUCE

Isn't there something comfortingly homely about the fish cake?

I don't know why that is. Maybe because it's a very domestic, economical dish – a thrifty way to use up leftover fish and potato. Isn't there a sort of old-fashionedness to the fish cake that's somehow reassuring? Or maybe it's just that they're something we have quite a bit as kids and not so much as adults, so they're seasoned with nostalgia. To be honest, any dish that stirs up that kind of emotion is a great thing to put on a plate.

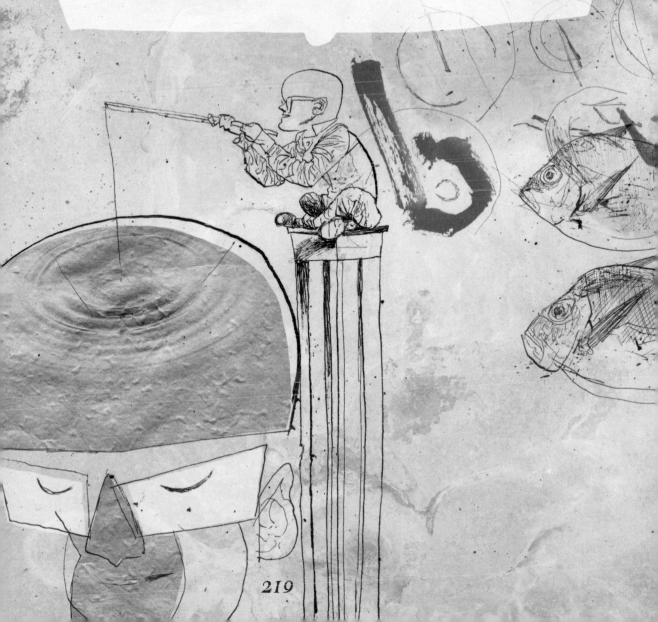

Fish Cakes with Tartare Sauce

MAKES 6

For the fish cakes
900g baking potatoes (about 3 large)
500g skinless fresh pollack fillets (or other white round fish)
500g skinless fresh salmon fillets
½ tsp paprika
Generous handful of fresh parsley
Generous handful of fresh chervil
Generous handful of fresh chives
Salt and black pepper

To coat and fry the fish cakes
150g plain flour
2 large eggs
150g **water**
150g panko breadcrumbs
Vegetable or sunflower oil, for deep-frying
Sea salt flakes

For the tartare sauce
2 banana shallots, peeled and finely chopped (about 30g)
275g mayonnaise
40g gherkins, finely chopped
40g drained capers, finely chopped
Finely grated zest and juice of 1 lemon
Generous handful of fresh parsley
Generous handful of fresh chervil
Generous handful of fresh chives

Preheat the oven to 200°C/Fan 180°C/Gas 6. Pierce the potatoes all over with a fork. Place them on a large baking tray and bake until tender, 1–1½ hours depending on their size.

While the potatoes are baking, make the tartare sauce. Soak the chopped shallots in cold **water** to cover for 10 minutes to mellow their flavour, then drain well and place in a medium bowl. Add the mayonnaise, gherkins, capers and lemon zest and juice and mix well to combine. Cover and set aside.

Once the potatoes are cool enough to handle, cut them in half and scoop out the soft, baked potato flesh. Pass through a fine-meshed sieve or potato ricer. You will need 500g mashed potato for this recipe.

Switch the oven to the grill setting at 140°C. Pat the fish fillets dry with kitchen paper and place them on a tray lined with baking paper. Grill in the oven until the fish is cooked, but not dry. Remove the fish from the tray and allow to cool completely.

A crunchy exterior adds a wonderful contrast to the softness that, for me at least, is a big part of the pleasure of a fish cake. I'm using panko breadcrumbs for true crunchaliciousness, but you can use whatever's to hand.

Of course, if you've got leftover mash, you can use it instead.

Use a probe thermometer if you have one. Ideally, you want the fish to reach 55°C.

Are there roasting juices left in the tray? Taste a little: isn't it full of fabulous fishy flavour? Don't you want that in your fish cakes? Hold on to them.

Continued on next page...

Transfer the fish to a bowl, saving the juices on the tray.
Add the mashed potato and paprika to the fish and mix well, adding some
of the juices to moisten. Finely chop the parsley, chervil and chives and
stir through, seasoning with salt and freshly ground black pepper.

Divide the mixture into 6 even portions. Shape each into a ball,
then flatten into a patty, about 3cm thick. Place on a tray, cover and refrigerate
to chill completely.

To coat the fish cakes, place the flour in a shallow bowl or small tray.
Whisk the eggs with the **water** in a second bowl. Put the breadcrumbs into
a third shallow bowl or small tray.

Roll each fish cake in the flour, gently tapping off any excess. Then dip into the
egg mixture and allow the excess egg to run off. Finally roll in the breadcrumbs
to coat all over. Set aside.

Heat the oil in a deep-fat fryer, or other large, deep, heavy-based pan (it must be
no more than half-filled) to 170°C. You will need to cook the fish cakes in batches.
Gently lower 2 or 3 of them into the hot oil and cook for about 8 minutes,
turning halfway through.

Remove the fish cakes with a slotted spoon, place on a tray lined with
kitchen paper to drain and sprinkle with sea salt flakes. Keep warm in a low oven
while you cook the rest.

Just before serving, finely chop the parsley, chervil and chives and stir through the
tartare sauce. Serve with the fish cakes.

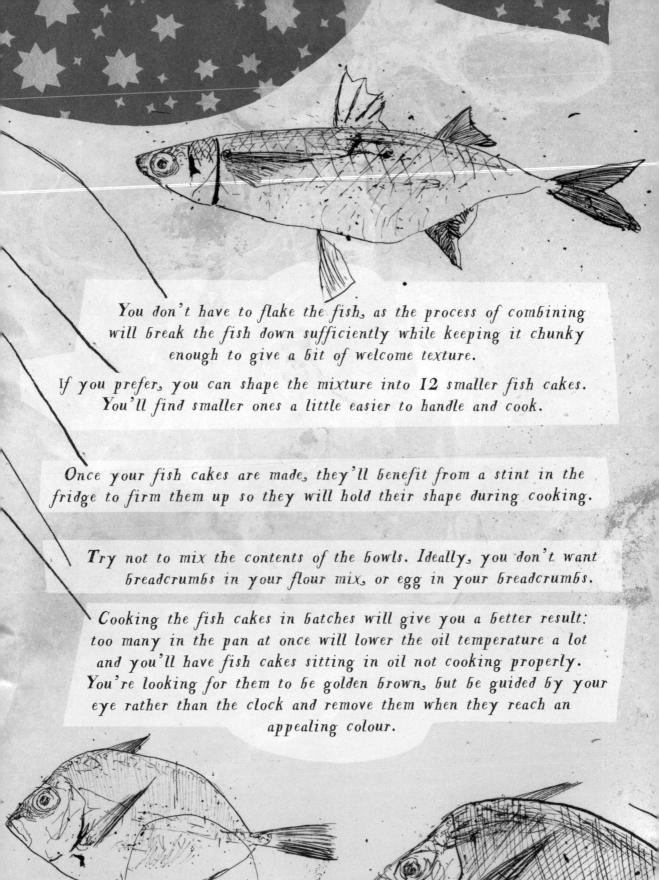

You don't have to flake the fish, as the process of combining will break the fish down sufficiently while keeping it chunky enough to give a bit of welcome texture.

If you prefer, you can shape the mixture into 12 smaller fish cakes. You'll find smaller ones a little easier to handle and cook.

Once your fish cakes are made, they'll benefit from a stint in the fridge to firm them up so they will hold their shape during cooking.

Try not to mix the contents of the bowls. Ideally, you don't want breadcrumbs in your flour mix, or egg in your breadcrumbs.

Cooking the fish cakes in batches will give you a better result: too many in the pan at once will lower the oil temperature a lot and you'll have fish cakes sitting in oil not cooking properly. You're looking for them to be golden brown, but be guided by your eye rather than the clock and remove them when they reach an appealing colour.

Mac 'n' Cheese

What's the ultimate comfort dish?

For a lot of us, it's got to be macaroni cheese. It is, of course, a classic dish of childhood, with a huge amount of nostalgia attached to it. But there's something about that dishful of rich, oozy generosity coated in melting cheese that melts most adults too.

Like any dish filled with emotion, it's one that everyone has a strong opinion about. I want lots of those little browned crisped-up bits, for a crunchy contrast, and I want the sauce to be sufficiently thick to really coat the pasta.

Many recipes for macaroni cheese achieve this by thickening with flour but, since starch masks flavour, I prefer to use cream cheese instead.

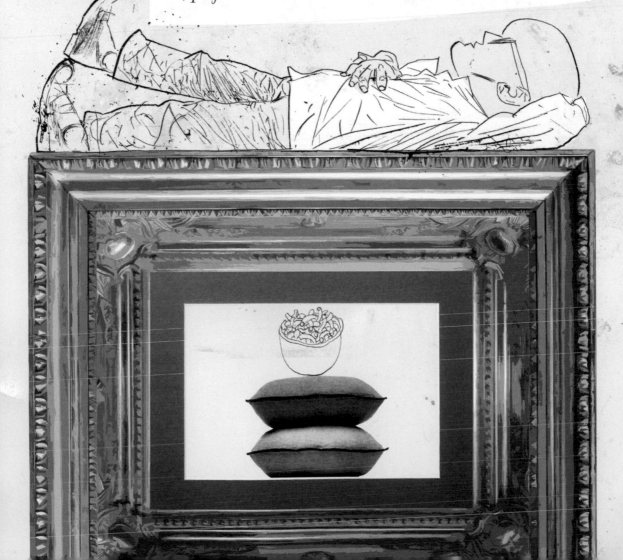

Mac 'n' Cheese

SERVES 4

40g salt
400g dried macaroni
300g whole milk
2 garlic cloves, peeled and crushed
200g cream cheese
240g finely grated Gruyère
240g finely grated Parmesan, plus an extra 40g to finish
Black pepper

Pour 4 litres **water** into a large pan, add the salt and bring to the boil. (If you haven't got a big enough pan, use 3 litres **water** and 30g salt.) Once the **water** is boiling, add the macaroni and cook until *al dente* (tender but with a bit of bite).

In the meantime, gently warm the milk and crushed garlic in a small pan over a low heat. Leave to infuse over a very low heat for 10 minutes, then strain the milk though a fine-meshed sieve into a large pan, discarding the garlic. Increase the heat and add the cream cheese. Stir to combine, then add the Gruyère and Parmesan and whisk well until all the cheese is melted and the sauce is smooth.

Preheat the oven grill to 200°C. As soon as the pasta is cooked, drain it, reserving a mugful of the cooking **water**.

Add the drained pasta to the cheese sauce and mix well to combine. Season with a little freshly ground black pepper and tip into a large, ovenproof dish (see below).

Scatter over the additional 40g Parmesan and place under the hot oven grill for about 8 minutes, until the mixture is bubbling and the surface is crispy and golden brown in places.

This is a dish you can prepare ahead of time to this point. Cover with foil and refrigerate until needed. When ready to serve, reheat, covered, in the oven preheated to 180°C/Fan 160°C/Gas 4 for 30 minutes, then remove the foil, top with the Parmesan and finish under the grill (as described in the final step).

The longer you let the garlic infuse into the milk, the more the garlic flavour will change and develop and deepen. Smell and taste the milk as you go, so you can get the strength of flavour you prefer.

It's handy to have a bit of the starchy pasta cooking water to hand to thin the sauce a little if necessary, without making it too runny.

A reasonably large dish is a good idea, if you like the crispy bits as much as I do, because a large surface area means more browned topping and more crispy bits.

'This being a classic, you may not want to muck about with it.
But this is a dish that you can really make your own.
Think about what you like: crispy bacon bits add texture, peas will lend sweetness, chopped herbs will add freshness. Ingredients that go well with cheese in other dishes will probably work here as well.
So, cauliflower is a no-brainer. Broccoli and blue cheese too.
Tomato, perhaps? You'll need to consider what needs cooking briefly first. But, other than that, feel free to attack the mac.'

COOK PASTA
LIKE AN ITALIAN

You're free, of course, to cook pasta any way you like but, let's face it, the Italians know a bit about how to do it, so why not try their approach? For them, pasta has to be al dente – soft but still with a bit of bite – and this is what they do to achieve that.

The ratio to hold in your head is 1:10:100 – per person, you need 1 litre water, 10g salt and 100g pasta. Having plenty of water stops the pasta from sticking, and the salt gives the pasta flavour and texture. (It might seem like a lot but, trust me, your pasta won't taste salty.)

Bring the water to the boil and add salt. Then add the pasta and swirl it around a little to encourage it not to stick together, then let it simmer. Many packets give a cooking time but I'd use this as a guideline only. Tasting is a much better guide than the clock as to when something is ready. Fish out a strand a couple of minutes before the packet says, bite into it and judge how near or far it is from how soft or hard you want it. You'll soon get an instinct for how long it'll take to soften to that state.

Taking charge of the pasta in this way, and tasting till it's ready, is a good way of getting exactly the texture you want. And in a mac 'n' cheese, that pasta will be a big part of what gives the dish its character. Those stiff dried tubes are hungry for water (which is part of why you've plunged them in water: to rehydrate them). If they go into the sauce still thirsty, they'll suck up the sauce instead and you might end up with something pretty dry. If they're already very soft they'll be reluctant to suck up anything and so won't really meld with the sauce. If you've got them al dente, however – which is straightforward if you keep monitoring and tasting – you'll get that magical amalgam of mac 'n' cheese. Mmmm.

CHILLI CON CARNE WITH SPICED CHOCOLATE

How about a bowl of red?

Isn't there something wonderful about putting a big bowl of chilli on the table and letting everybody help themselves? It's a spicy, filling, big-flavoured dish that encourages a sense of community. Real comfort food, whether you serve it with rice or on a baked potato or with tortilla chips on the side for everyone to dip 'n' munch.

The fact that something's considered a classic is no reason not to play around with it. Respect rather than reverence is the name of the game, as far as I'm concerned. So long as you stay true to the spirit of the dish, you're still cooking the classic. Notions of authenticity can get in the way of creativity. To my chilli I like to add a little spiced chocolate. Some people might consider this a step too far, but chilli con carne's origins straddle the border between Texas and Mexico. I've been to chilli cook-offs in America where competitors have added cocoa powder or chocolate, and Mexico has a long tradition of putting chocolate in its mole sauce, so why not?

Chilli con Carne with Spiced Chocolate

SERVES 4–6

For the chilli con carne
6 tbsp olive oil
450g beef mince
1 large onion, peeled and finely chopped
2 star anise
3 garlic cloves, peeled and crushed
1 red chilli, deseeded and finely chopped
2 tbsp concentrated tomato purée
375g red wine
400g tin chopped tomatoes
500g beef stock
400g tin red kidney beans, drained and rinsed
155g piquillo peppers (drained from a jar), roughly chopped
Salt and black pepper

For the spiced chocolate
120g dark chocolate (70% cocoa solids)
50g unsalted butter
2 tbsp olive oil
1½ tsp ground cumin
1½ tsp ground coriander
1 tsp chilli powder
1 tbsp tomato ketchup
1 tbsp mushroom ketchup or Worcestershire sauce

To serve
About 100g spiced chocolate (from above)
Cooked rice

Heat 3 tbsp olive oil in a large pan over a high heat.
Once smoking hot, brown the mince in batches until evenly and deeply coloured.
Remove the cooked mince with a slotted spoon and transfer to a bowl.

Add a dash of **water** to the pan to deglaze it, stirring and scraping the bottom of the pan to loosen any flavourful bits that are stuck. Tip the liquid into the bowl of mince.

Reduce the heat to medium and add the remaining 3 tbsp oil to the pan.
Add the onion and star anise and cook until the onion is softened and starting to colour. Add the garlic and chilli and cook, stirring regularly, for a further 5 minutes.

Add the tomato purée and cook for another 5 minutes (the mixture will become brick-red in colour).

Return the cooked mince and all the juices from the bowl to the pan and pour in the red wine. Simmer over a medium heat for about 25 minutes until reduced by two-thirds.

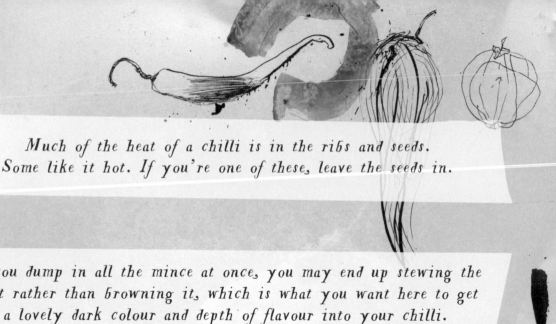

Much of the heat of a chilli is in the ribs and seeds.
Some like it hot. If you're one of these, leave the seeds in.

If you dump in all the mince at once, you may end up stewing the
meat rather than browning it, which is what you want here to get
a lovely dark colour and depth of flavour into your chilli.

These bits are full of tasty browned
Maillard flavours that you don't want to lose.

Cooking onions with star anise is a neat technique
I developed for boosting the 'meaty' notes of a dish.

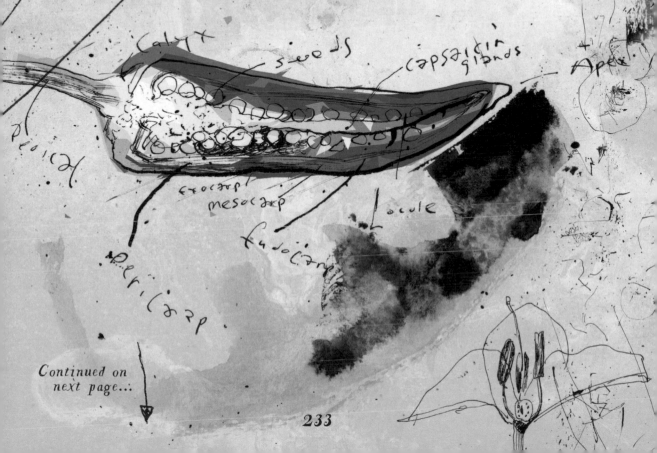

Continued on
next page...

Now add the chopped tomatoes and beef stock. Bring back to a simmer and reduce the heat to medium-low. Leave to simmer uncovered until the mixture is thickened. This can take up to 90 minutes.

While the chilli is cooking, prepare the spiced chocolate. Line a small tray with baking paper. Break up the chocolate into small pieces and place in a heatproof bowl set over a pan of barely simmering **water** (bain-marie). Once melted, whisk in the butter, then add all the remaining ingredients, mixing well to combine. Pour onto the lined tray and leave to set.

Once the chilli is cooked, stir in the kidney beans and chopped Piquillo peppers and warm through.

Break up 100g of the set spiced chocolate and add to the chilli, allowing it to melt in. Remove and discard the star anise and season with salt and freshly ground black pepper. Serve the chilli with cooked rice.

This is a dish you can make in advance and keep covered in the fridge for a couple of days, ready to gently reheat before serving. You could even make a larger batch and freeze portions for future meals.

You want the water to have barely the blip of a bubble to ensure the chocolate doesn't overheat and go grainy. It's not a disaster if that happens but the texture won't be as delightfully smooth.

You can, of course, add as much or as little of the spiced chocolate as you like. We suggest 15g spiced chocolate per 200g portion of chilli, but it's up to you. The chilli will still taste really good if you leave it out altogether.

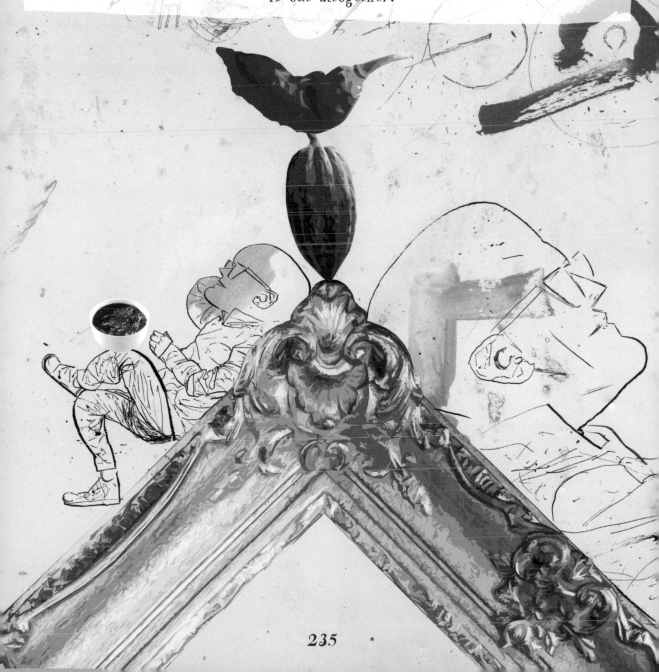

ROAST POTATOES

Roast Chicken and Gravy, Yorkshire Puddings

In the end isn't a roast all about the roast potatoes?

While we all love a roast, I reckon that deep down we all have this secret shared belief that the best bit of any roast is the roast potato. Of course, there's a majesty to a tender, juicy, aromatic chicken with a lovely browned skin. Of course, a big-flavoured gravy makes a difference. But no matter how delicious everything else is, if the roasties aren't quite there, then we're not quite satisfied.

That's probably part of the reason I got a little bit obsessed about getting roast potatoes with exactly the texture I wanted: crispy and crunchy on the outside; soft and fluffy on the inside. So, if that's how you like your potatoes, you're in for a treat.

Roast Potatoes

2kg Maris Piper potatoes
Salt
Vegetable oil (or melted goose fat, duck fat, lard), for roasting
3 sprigs of fresh thyme
6 garlic cloves, peeled

Peel the potatoes and cut them into even-sized large chunks. Immerse the potatoes
in a bowl of cold **water** as you prepare them to prevent browning.

Rinse the potatoes in a colander under cold running **water** until the **water** runs
clear, to remove excess starch.

Fill a large pan with lightly salted **water** and add the potatoes. Bring to the boil,
then reduce the heat to a simmer and cook for 25 minutes until tender.
Drain them very well in a colander, then spread out on a large wire rack set over
a tray. Allow to cool.

In the meantime, preheat the oven to 200°C/Fan 180°C/Gas 6. Select a large
roasting tray, big enough to take all the potatoes spread out in a single layer.
Add enough oil (or melted fat) to the roasting tray to create a shallow layer,
about 5mm deep.

Lay the potatoes out carefully in the roasting tray, including all the smaller,
broken-up pieces (they make delicious ultra-crispy bits), and roast in the oven
for 20 minutes.

Turn the potatoes a little and roast them for an additional 20 minutes
or until firmed up and lightly golden on all sides.

Turn the potatoes once more, especially the sides that look like they may need
more time. Scatter over the thyme and use the back of a knife to smash the garlic
cloves. Add these to the tray and return to the oven for another 20 minutes.
The potatoes will be golden and crispy.

Season the roast potatoes with salt and serve immediately, to retain
their crispness.

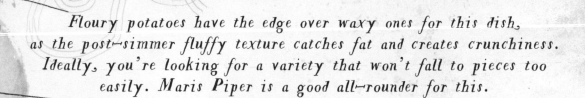

Floury potatoes have the edge over waxy ones for this dish, as the post—simmer fluffy texture catches fat and creates crunchiness. Ideally, you're looking for a variety that won't fall to pieces too easily. Maris Piper is a good all—rounder for this.

These could be thirds or quarters, depending on the size of the potatoes. Those pointy corners are good, anyway, as they can catch fat and create crispiness.

You will notice that the potatoes have not only softened, but they also look a little translucent. Some may show cracks, or even have broken up a little. This is a key part of the process: those cracks are where fat can collect, which is what creates that crunchy exterior.

Overcrowding the pan tends to hinder browning and crisping, so aim for a bit of space between each spud.

At this point, take a good look at your potatoes. Are they firm, with a harder skin, and golden all over? If not, you'll need to return them to the oven until they are, before going on to the next stage.

Roast Chicken and Gravy

SERVES 4–6

For the chicken
1 large chicken
Salt
2 sprigs of fresh thyme
5 garlic cloves, peeled; 2 smashed and 3 sliced
2 carrots, peeled and sliced
1 onion, peeled and sliced
2 celery stalks, finely sliced
6 mushrooms, finely sliced
2 tbsp olive oil

For the gravy
Trimmings and veg (from the roasting tray)
1 tsp concentrated tomato purée
500g chicken stock or **water**
30g Bisto chicken gravy granules
4 sprigs of fresh thyme
Sherry vinegar, to taste
Salt and black pepper

Preheat the oven to 160°C/Fan 140°C/Gas 3.

To prepare the chicken, remove the wishbone and any trussing. Open the legs and remove the wings, parson's nose and any excess fat. Reserve these trimmings for later. Season the whole chicken with salt, including the cavity. Put the thyme and smashed garlic inside the cavity.

Chop the reserved chicken trimmings (wings etc.) into smaller pieces and spread out in a large roasting tray along with the carrots, onion, celery, mushrooms, and sliced garlic.

Rub 1 tbsp olive oil all over the chicken, then sit it on top of the trimmings and veg in the roasting tray. Roast in the oven for 30 minutes.

Take the tray from the oven and insert a probe thermometer into the thickest part of the chicken (thigh and breast) to check the temperature. It should registers 60°C; if necessary return the tray to the oven and roast for a little longer, then test again.

Once the temperature reaches 60°C, remove the whole chicken from the tray and set it aside on a plate, covered with foil, to rest. Increase the oven temperature to 200°C/Fan 180°C/Gas 6.

Return the roasting tray with all the trimmings and vegetables to the oven and continue to cook until lightly golden. Stir through the tomato purée and roast for an additional 5–10 minutes. Remove the tray from the oven and pour in 100g stock or **water**. Stir well to deglaze the pan and loosen any sticky bits. Pour the contents of the tray into a large pan.

A digital probe thermometer is a really useful piece of kitchen kit that's not particularly expensive. It will more or less guarantee you end up with a succulent chicken – or turkey at Xmas, for that matter.

Caramelising vegetables like this will produce a rich flavour. Give it a try: they should be completely soft and have a meaty, roasted flavour.

These bits are full of plenty of caramelised flavour so why waste them?

Continued on next page...

Increase the heat of the oven once again, to its maximum setting. Rub 1 tbsp oil all over the chicken and place it back in the roasting tray. Return to the oven until the chicken is warmed through and the skin is browned, about 10–15 minutes.

Meanwhile, to make the gravy, bring the pan to a simmer and let it simmer for 5 minutes. Pick out and discard any chicken bones, then strain the liquor through a large sieve into a clean pan, pushing as much of the veg through as possible. Discard the contents of the sieve. Add the rest of the stock or **water** to the strained mixture and bring to a simmer. Whisk in the gravy granules and continue to whisk until you are happy with the consistency.

Remove the pan from the heat, add the thyme sprigs and set aside to infuse for 5 minutes. Pick out and discard the thyme, then season the gravy with a little sherry vinegar, salt and freshly ground black pepper as needed.

Carve the roast chicken and serve with the gravy, roast potatoes, Yorkshire puddings if serving, and vegetables of your choice.

You can also get creative spicing the chicken. Chinese five-spice, curry powder, cumin, paprika are all excellent options. Even ground cinnamon would be exciting. Smoked salt and chilli powder can also be considered. Any of these could go inside or outside the bird.

This vegetable purée will help thicken the gravy.

You like your gravy thicker? Just add a bit more Bisto.

And finally, one little tip: while carving, check out the two little round morsels of dark meat known as the 'oysters', which are found on the back of the bird near the thigh. They're pieces of absolute deliciousness that are often overlooked. (The French call them 'Les sot-l'y-laisse', which roughly translates as 'what the fool leaves in place'.) You could be generous and serve them to others, or invoke chef's privilege and keep them for yourself. After your stint in the kitchen, I'd say you've earned them.

Yorkshire Puddings

160g whole milk
100g plain flour
2 large eggs (about 128g)
½ tsp salt
Vegetable oil for cooking

Have ready a Yorkshire pudding tray with 2–3cm deep holes. (Alternatively, you could make more smaller puddings in non-stick muffin trays.)

To make the batter, whisk the milk and flour together in a bowl, ensuring it is free from lumps. Add the eggs and salt and whisk well to combine and make a smooth batter. Transfer to a jug, cover and leave in the fridge until needed.

When you are ready to cook, preheat the oven to 230°C/Fan 210°C/Gas 8. Place the Yorkshire pudding tray on the middle shelf of the oven to heat up.

Once the tray is hot, add a little oil to each hole of the tray (about a 5mm depth) and return the tray to the oven.

Once the oil is smoking hot, pour in the batter (about 1cm deep in each hole). Immediately place the tray back in the oven and bake for 15–20 minutes until the puddings have puffed up and turned golden brown.

Allow the Yorkshire puddings to cool slightly before removing from the tray.

It's not a bad idea to let the batter rest a while, as this allows the gluten to relax, which will help the puddings to rise. You can even make it a day or two in advance and store it in the fridge.

Although the top of the oven is the hottest place, the middle shelf is the best place for the puddings because they'll rise spectacularly and you don't want them reaching the roof of the oven.

Properly hot oil is the key to the Yorkshire pudding. First, it provides a protective layer that helps prevent the batter from sticking to the pan. Second, that heat cooks the batter quickly, encouraging it to rise up into full fluffiness.

You want to do this quickly and efficiently, so that the temperature doesn't dip much and heat transfers from the oil to the batter quickly to begin making it rise. Avoid shaking the tray and mixing the oil and batter together, which could result in greasy Yorkshire puddings.

'Do you want a Yorkshire pud with a bigger flavour? Try whisking a spoonful or so of mustard into the batter.'

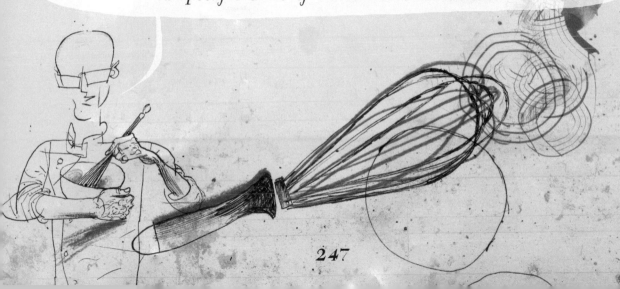

7

A Bit on the Side

*Do you want a sauce, dip or condiment
with that?*

Japanese Special Sauce 'Umamilicious'

•

Raitziki

•

Tomato Compote Ketchup

•

Hemp Satay

•

Kimchi Miso Dressing

JAPANESE SPECIAL SAUCE
'UMAMILICIOUS'

How many tastes are there?

For a long time it was thought there were only four: salty, sweet, sour and bitter.

However, in the early 1900s, a Japanese professor started looking into kombu (giant kelp, which had been an ingredient in Japanese cuisine for centuries but was little known in the West). He discovered it contained monosodium glutamate, which has its own distinctive taste, which he named 'umami'. Western scientists were at first doubtful that this was a taste in its own right, but in 2001 a biologist proved that we do have specific taste receptors for MSG.

And then there were five...

Since then, umami has become a more familiar term, and introducing it to dishes has become an invaluable part of the cook's arsenal – bringing depth and complexity and a big boost of savoury deliciousness. There are many ways to do this: you could simply sprinkle on some MSG. You could incorporate ingredients that have umami, like anchovies, ketchup or Parmesan. But what if you could bottle that taste, ready to dash a splash of savouriness when needed?
Well, this sauce does exactly that – it's a handy way to add some umami to all sorts of dishes. One day I'm going to bottle it commercially, but until then why not make your own?

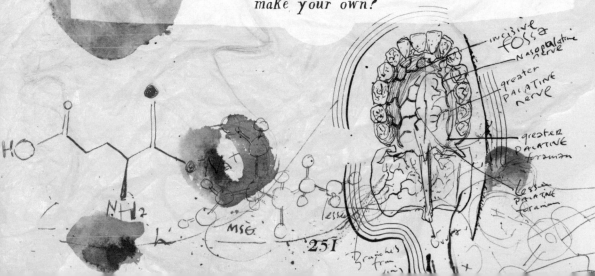

Japanese Special Sauce 'Umamilicious'

MAKES ABOUT 250G

2 litres dashi
20g crushed or roughly chopped dried shiitake mushrooms
2g bonito flakes
3g white soy or light soy sauce
3g tamari
3g mirin

Pour the dashi into a pan, add the shiitake mushrooms and bring to a simmer over a medium heat. Continue to simmer until the liquid is reduced right down, to one tenth of the original volume. Remove from the heat, add the bonito flakes and set aside to infuse for 2 minutes only.

Strain the mixture through a fine-meshed sieve into a bowl, using the back of a spoon to squeeze out as much liquid and flavour as possible from the shiitake and bonito flakes. Discard the contents of the sieve. You should have approximately 240g liquid.

Stir through the soy, tamari and mirin to season the sauce.

Store the sauce in a sealed sterilised bottle in the fridge and it will keep for up to several weeks. Add a few drops to soups, stocks, sauces, salad dressings or indeed any dish that will benefit from umami flavouring.

It's important to use regular dashi and not shiro-dashi, which is highly concentrated and will result in a sauce that is far too salty.

Dashi, shiitake, bonito, soy, tamari, mirin – all of these things are rich in umami, but each expresses it in a different way. Why not taste each as you go?

You'll build a really three-dimensional flavour-portrait of this taste that you can bank in your memory for future cooking. Slurp a little soy sauce, what impressions do you get? Taste a 'shroom shard: what similarities does it have to soy sauce, and what differences? You're probably getting a saltiness and a savouriness. Sometimes that umami taste is so intense it can make people tingle or shiver, or cause the hairs on the back of their neck to prickle.

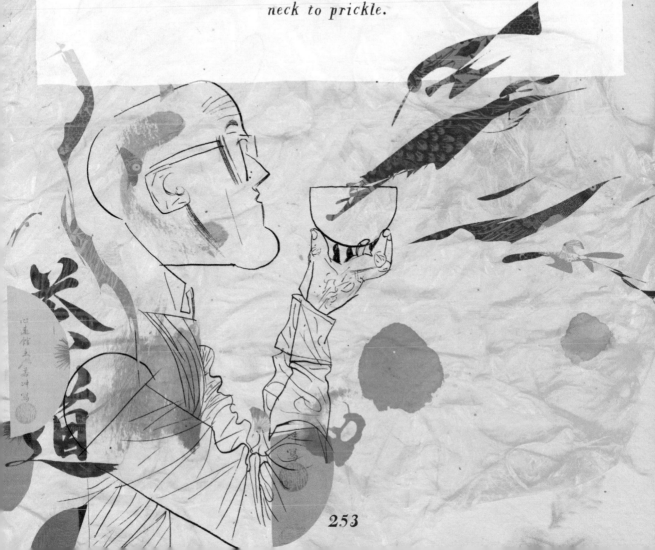

RAITZIKI

What's the difference between raita and tzatziki?

The answer is: very little. One's from India, the other from Greece, but both are, in essence, a combination of cucumber, yoghurt and fragrant herbs, perhaps with a spritz of citrus. Some say tzatziki uses thicker yoghurt. Some say raita favours coriander while tzatziki typically uses mint, dill or parsley. Do such distinctions matter? Not really, since either way you end up with something delightfully fresh and cooling that can act as an accompaniment to all sorts of dishes.

I guess what this shows us is that no recipe is set in stone and that in cuisine there are no hard and fast distinctions. It's all about being creative and making something your own. So, I've taken the bits I like from raita and tzatziki to come up with... raitziki? See what you think. Maybe eventually you'll take it somewhere else and rename it yet again.

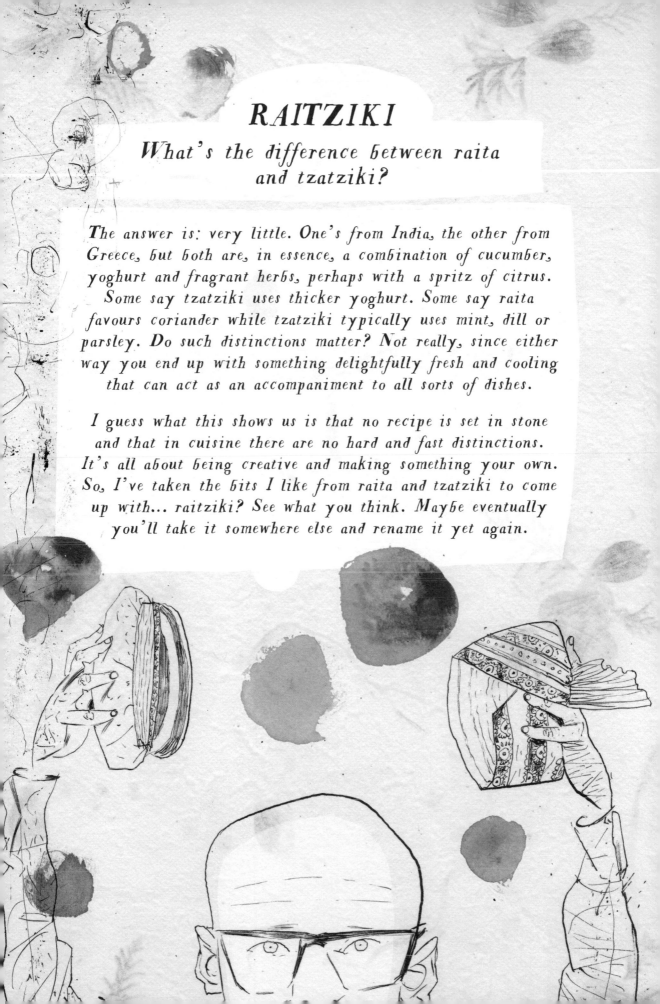

Raitziki

MAKES ABOUT 540G

1 cucumber
300g hung (or extra-thick) yoghurt (see page 259)
Generous pinch of salt
Finely grated zest and juice of 1 lime
20g fresh coriander

Coarsely grate the cucumber and place in a fine-meshed sieve to drain off the excess liquid.

Tip the drained cucumber into a bowl and add the yoghurt, salt and the lime zest and juice.

Chop the coriander, add to the bowl and mix well to combine.

Fresh, sharp, zingy lime brings the dish alive.
You might want to go easy on it, adding the zest first,
then squeezing in the juice and tasting as you go.
It needs a gentle hand if it's not to overwhelm the other ingredients.

If you don't like coriander, you can explore using other herbs – mint,
dill, parsley or some combo of any or all of these. As I said at the
beginning, there are no rules and you can really make this dish your
own. Raiding different 'traditional' elements from tzatziki or raita
might be a start. What about cayenne in there, or ginger,
or a pinch of cumin...?

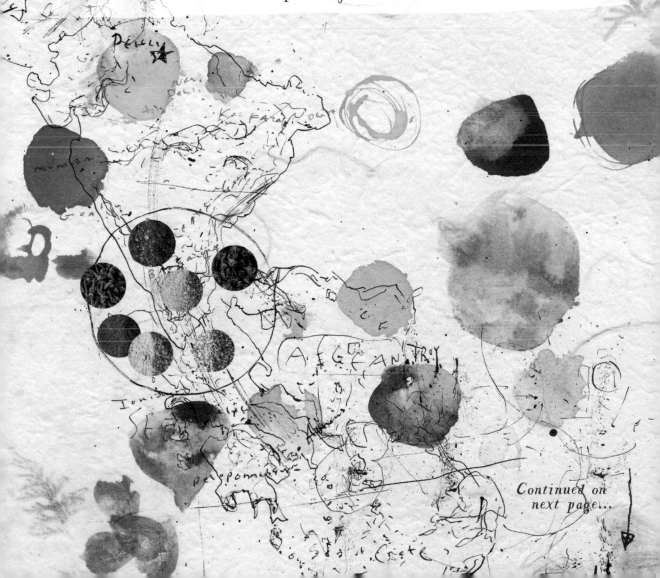

Continued on
next page...

'Isn't this another good example of a quantum dish? In quantum physics, an entity can be a wave or a particle and both possibilities co-exist until we try to pin it down to one or the other. And it's the same here – your yoghurt can be both Greek and Indian until we feel the need to name it.'

'On a slightly less nerdy note, extra-thick yoghurt is best here because the liquid from the cucumber will thin the yoghurt down. You want a good dollop on your plate, not a sloppy puddle.

You can make your own: line a sieve with a piece of muslin and set it over a saucepan or bowl. Empty the yoghurt into the muslin and enclose it in the material like a pouch, twisting the ends together. Squeeze out excess water then put a lid on top and place the whole set-up in the fridge overnight so the yoghurt can continue to drain. The next day, the mixture will be firmer, almost ricotta-like – useful in any dish that calls for a firmer yoghurt texture, such as Chicken tikka kebab or Lamb curry on pages 186 and 188.'

TOMATO COMPOTE KETCHUP

What inspires your cooking?

One of the beauties of cooking is the way recipes get handed down, changed, and handed on again. A culinary heritage and a link from one person to another via food. Human connectivity.

The inspiration for this ketchup is the Bois Boudran sauce created by Michel Roux Senior, who died in 2020. Michel was my neighbour in Bray, running the incredible Waterside Inn, the first restaurant outside France to hold three Michelin stars for 25 years. From the moment I first opened The Fat Duck in 1995 Michel was completely supportive, providing me with a replacement chocolate cake after the complicated one I'd created for a demanding customer slipped off the fridge onto the floor; and even grabbing the microphone from me after my presentation at a Madrid gastronomic congress to say that he felt like a father figure to me and was proud of what I'd done. He is much missed.

Tomato Compote Ketchup

MAKES ABOUT 265G

1 shallot, peeled and finely chopped
130g Tomato compote (page 174)
60g olive oil
1 tbsp sherry vinegar
2 tsp Worcestershire sauce
1 tsp soy sauce
1 tsp wholegrain or Dijon mustard
Finely grated zest of ½ lemon
Salt and black pepper
Small handful of fresh tarragon and parsley leaves

Put the chopped shallot into a bowl, pour on cold **water** to cover and leave to soak for 5–10 minutes (to mellow the harsh taste). Drain well.

In a bowl, combine the shallot with the tomato compote, olive oil, sherry vinegar, Worcestershire sauce, soy sauce, mustard and lemon zest. Season the mixture with salt and freshly ground black pepper.

Finely chop the tarragon (about 2g) and parsley (about 1g) and stir through the sauce.

Store in a sealed sterilised jar in the fridge, where it will keep for up to a week.

This sauce is most flavourful at room temperature so, if you remember, take it out of the fridge an hour or two in advance. It's delicious in any dish that needs a bit of sharp, punchy tomato sauce.

'This is another recipe that makes great use of the full-flavoured tomato compote that's the backbone of my Ratatouille (page 173). For other dishes that feature the compote, see Tomato and coffee muffins (page 65) and Pasta puttanesca (page 179).'

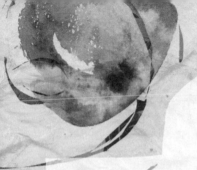

HEMP SATAY
Going with the grain?

One of the positive aspects of our concern about the fragility of our planet, and the need to interact with it in more mindful and sustainable ways, is a reignited interest in healthy 'old' ingredients such as spelt, barley, millet, farro, teff, sorghum, freekeh, amaranth and kamut. And a growing interest in healthy 'new' ones too. A few years back, ingredients like quinoa, chia seeds, edamame and tempeh weren't on many people's radar. Now, increasingly, they're available in supermarkets, appearing in recipes and becoming part of our diet, which is incredibly exciting.

Hemp is just such an ingredient. Even though it was possibly the first crop cultivated by humankind, it hasn't featured much in the modern diet. Yet these seeds are full of fibre, antioxidants, minerals, vitamins and protein, so they offer plenty of health benefits and are a particularly good resource for plant-based cooking. There's a deep savouriness to the flavour that I really appreciate.

Hemp Satay

100g shelled (hulled) hemp seeds
1½ tsp soft brown sugar
90g full-fat coconut milk
55g tamarind paste
Finely grated zest and juice of ½ lime, plus extra if needed
2 tsp soy sauce, plus extra if needed

Preheat the oven to 200°C/Fan 180°C/Gas 6.

Spread the hemp seeds out on a baking tray and toast in the oven for about 10–12 minutes until golden, rotating the tray and mixing the seeds around halfway through.

Remove from the oven and tip the seeds onto a plate. Leave to cool for 10 minutes then tip into a blender.

Add all the remaining ingredients to the blender and blitz to a smooth paste. Taste the mixture and if you feel it needs more acidity add a little extra lime juice. If you think you need to up the umami salty flavour, add a little more soy.

Store in an airtight container in the fridge. It will keep for up to a week.

This is enough for four people to share
as a dip alongside grilled chicken.

There's a deeply individual range of flavours and
textures here that are worth trying before you add
them. The saltiness of that soy. The sweet/sour
pastiness of tamarind. Smooth, rich coconut milk.
Fresh, sharp, acidic lime zest. Perhaps you can
begin to imagine how these might all come together.

'How loose or firm you have your satay it is up
to you. I like a dippable consistency, like a pesto.
If you feel your sauce is too firm, you can
add a little water without compromising the
flavour too much.'

'Traditionally, this is a dipping sauce for skewers
or kebabs. It also makes a nice dressing for stir-fries
or Asian salads. A hassle-free way of trying it out
would be to fry or grill some chicken strips to dip
in it. Or, why not try it with one of the "new"
ingredients I mentioned: get a 200g packet of tempeh
(cooked, fermented soy beans – sort of like tofu but
with a firmer texture and nutty flavour), cut it into
strips and marinate it for a while in a few teaspoonfuls
of soy sauce plus a teaspoonful or so of sesame oil.
Then fry in a pan in a little oil for a couple of minutes
and you're ready to serve with the satay
on the side.'

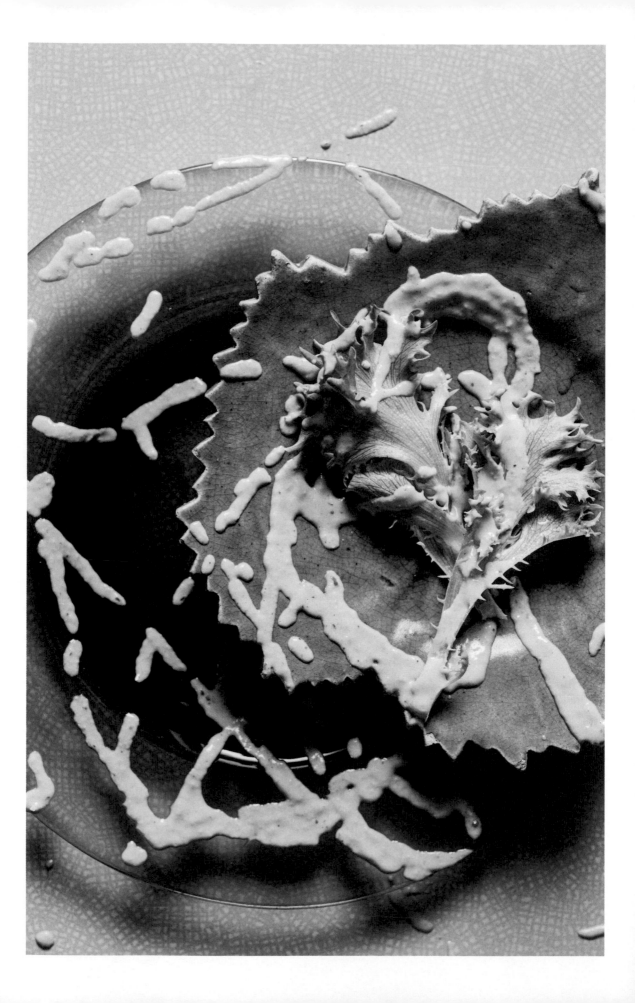

KIMCHI MISO DRESSING

What can I make with kimchi?

This is another opportunity to use that incredible kimchi you've lovingly encouraged to a state of fantastic fermented goodness and deliciousness. It's basically a vegan mayonnaise that's incredibly versatile – you can dress salads with it. Dip crudités in it. Spread it on sandwiches. Or use it anywhere you want a bit of mayo action.

'What do you mean you haven't made kimchi yet? It's probably the most fun you can have with a cabbage leaf. Check out the Fermentation Station on page 272 and you'll see what I mean.'

Kimchi Miso Dressing

MAKES ABOUT 375G

90g Kimchi (page 277)
50g miso paste
120g silken tofu, drained
1 tbsp rice wine vinegar, plus extra if needed
Salt
80g vegetable oil

Put the kimchi, miso paste, tofu and rice wine vinegar into a blender.
Add a pinch of salt and blitz until smooth.

Slowly drizzle in the oil as you continue to blitz, until the mixture emulsifies
like a mayonnaise.

Taste and adjust the seasoning if you need to.

This dressing will keep well in a sealed jar in the fridge for up to a week.
It's delicious with salads!

Silken tofu is a good replacement for eggs in dishes like this one. On its own it's quite bland but it's good at taking on flavours and, as the name suggests, it helps create a lovely creamy silky mouthfeel, which is what we're going for here.

Are you happy with the balance? You might want to add a little more vinegar if you prefer a sharper finish.

8

The Fermentation Station

*Ready to get to grips with the gut-brain
and the brain-gut?*

Kimchi

•

Kimchi Potato Cake 'Disco Bonito'

•

Amazake Drink

•

Heston's Soda Bar

Kombucha

Lime and Green Peppercorn Kombucha

Orange and Thyme Kombucha

Kombucha Cola

Coke Float 'Brown Cow'

Kombucha Beer

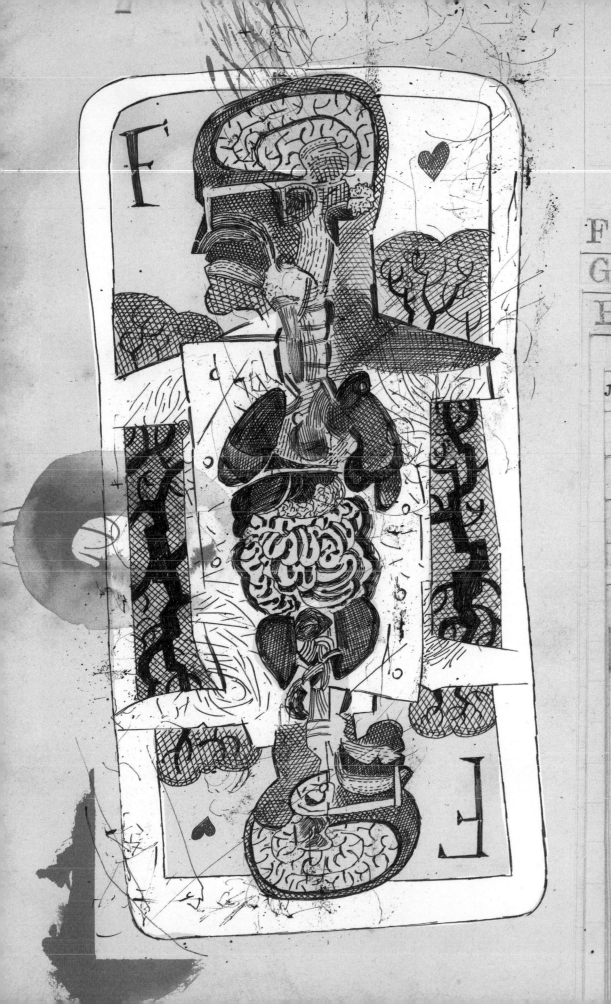

F
G
H
I
J
K
L
M
N
O
P
Q
R
S
T
U
V
W
X
Y
Z

FERMENTATION EXPLORATION

I spent 25 years looking at food and cooking from the outside in, trying to impose what now seems a rather arbitrary notion of perfection. Increasingly I find I now want to look at food and cooking from the inside out – exploring, for example, how our microbiome can influence more than just our physical well-being. How the gut talks to the brain. And the brain to the gut. There's a universe inside us and food plays a vital role in it. It can help determine our mood, our emotions, our mental well-being.

Fermented foods such as kimchi, kombucha and koji are being highlighted as potentially very good for our guts because they're probiotic (i.e. full of healthy bacteria). Scientists are still exploring the benefits, but there's strong evidence that these microbes maintain the gut lining, regulate immunity, control inflammation, suppress some 'bad' bacteria and act as a sort of natural antibiotic, as well as helping us absorb nutrients and vitamins from our food.

The research may be in its infancy but, if you're interested in food and cooking, why not explore what fermented food is all about? If nothing else, you'll discover a great set of textures and bright sharp flavours, and maybe you'll give your gut a boost into the bargain. I've certainly been exploring this area for a number of years in my development lab, to the point where my chefs have sometimes come to think of it as 'The Fermentation Station'. Why don't we visit it?

KIMCHI

How about some entry-level fermentation?

Most of us are probably familiar with fermentation, mainly in the form of yoghurt, but there's a whole world of fermented foods to explore, from sauerkraut and pickled fruit and veg to tempeh, kefir and kombucha.

'You'll find kefir in the Banana and parsley smoothie on page 55, Gut-friendly beetroot soup on page III, and Popcorn popcorn chicken on page 153.'

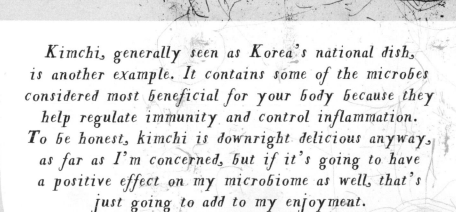

Kimchi, generally seen as Korea's national dish, is another example. It contains some of the microbes considered most beneficial for your body because they help regulate immunity and control inflammation. To be honest, kimchi is downright delicious anyway, as far as I'm concerned, but if it's going to have a positive effect on my microbiome as well, that's just going to add to my enjoyment.

Kimchi

MAKES 1 BATCH

2 large heads of Chinese cabbage (or Chinese leaf)
About 110g non-iodised salt
20g peeled and finely grated garlic cloves
10g peeled and finely grated fresh ginger
1 red chilli, finely sliced
40g honey
40g gochugaru (Korean chilli powder)
2 tbsp fish sauce
400g peeled and trimmed daikon

Wash the cabbage and cut lengthways into 8 wedges. Layer the cabbage leaves in a bowl, sprinkling the salt between all the layers. Cover and leave at room temperature for 5–6 hours. It's a good idea to turn the cabbage 2 or 3 times. You will notice how the cabbage becomes tender and malleable; it shouldn't snap. Rinse the leaves under cold, running **water** and squeeze out any excess moisture.

Place the cabbage leaves in a clean bowl and add the garlic, ginger and chilli, along with the honey, chilli powder and fish sauce. Massage this mixture into the cabbage leaves.

Cut the daikon lengthways into 4 wedges, then slice thinly. Add the sliced daikon to the cabbage mix and combine well.

Transfer the mixture to a clean 1.5–2-litre container, such as a Mason or Kilner jar, and pack it in tightly. Tuck in the softer leaves and fold the wedges in half to fit them into the jar.

Cover the surface of the mixture with cling film and compress down to remove any air, adding a suitable weight to keep the veg submerged. (Many fermentation kits contain the appropriate gear, including weights. Alternatively, the kimchi can be made in a sealed bag.)

Leave the jar at room temperature until the kimchi starts to smell and taste sour. It should be ready after about 7 days. Be sure to open the jar once a day to release the gasses. If you spot any mould, the kimchi is unfortunately a ruined batch and must be discarded.

I've given an approximate quantity of salt, but for the most precise approach, after trimming your cabbages, weigh the yield. The salt should be 5 per cent of the cabbage weight.

You're taking part in a human tradition stretching back hundreds of years. Korean families used to prepare kimchi in earthenware pots that would then be buried in the ground and allowed to ripen, possibly over long periods of time. For me, the connectedness that food can bring about is an exciting and moving part of cooking.

I find there's a pleasurable dimension to this – a sense of having nurtured something or brought it into being. Maybe, like me, you'll find you develop an almost emotional connection with your cabbage in its jar, checking in on it every so often to monitor its progress.

'Fancy a kimchi that isn't spicy? Just leave out the chillies and the chilli powder.'

KIMCHI POTATO CAKE 'DISCO BONITO'

Was bonito born to boogie?

I love this dish, partly because it's delicious and very
comforting, and partly because of what happened
when I was eating it with my development team outdoors.
As the plates were put on the table, the heat from
the dish meant the feather-light bonito flakes lifted
and began breezily bobbing about.
We had put on some sounds
(probably Ash - Live for Beirut)
and it was just as if they were dancing
in time to the music.
(With the cicadas providing extra percussion.)

I got very excited about this because I remembered once
watching a video clip that used music and moving images to
demonstrate how our brain likes to see patterns in things,
to the extent that it'll make them even where they
don't strictly exist. Why not find out for yourself?

Make the dish,
put on some tunes
and check out
the bonito flakes.

Are they dancing
to the music?...

Kimchi Potato Cake 'Disco Bonito'

SERVES 1-2

For the kimchi potato cake
2 medium potatoes
Salt
50g Kimchi (page 277), roughly chopped
½ spring onion, finely sliced
10g peeled fresh ginger, finely chopped
1 tsp soy sauce
1 tbsp vegetable oil

To garnish
Okonomiyaki (or HP) sauce
Mayonnaise
Sliced spring onion
Furikake
A handful of katsuobushi (dried and smoked bonito flakes)

Peel and grate the potatoes into a bowl; you should ideally have 180g grated potato. Scatter over 2 pinches of salt and set aside for 10 minutes.

In the meantime, rinse a clean tea towel under cold, running **water** and wring out all excess **water**. Tip the potatoes onto the tea towel and wrap the tea towel around them. Squeeze the potatoes strongly over the sink to remove all excess moisture; you should be left with about 115g grated, drained potato.

Tip the potatoes into a bowl and stir through the chopped kimchi, spring onion, ginger and soy, mixing well to combine.

Heat the oil in a good-quality, flat, non-stick frying pan over a moderate heat for 2 minutes. Add the potato mixture to the centre of the pan and press down with the back of a spoon to spread the mixture out until about 12cm in diameter and 1cm high.

Leave to cook for 4–5 minutes to allow the base to form a crust, which helps hold the delicate mixture together. Use a large spatula or fish slice to carefully flip the potato cake to cook the underside. (Alternatively, you could place a plate over the cake and flip the pan over, before sliding the cake back into the pan.)

Gently press down to ensure an even cook and leave on the heat for another 4–5 minutes to ensure the potatoes cook through sufficiently.

Serve with a drizzle or scattering of the suggested garnishes.

At this stage, you've already got what you need for the classic Swiss dish, rösti. So you could just season it and put it in a pan. And maybe sometimes, that'll be all you want to do – a rösti is a very satisfying, comforting dish...

...But if you take a look at the ingredients you're about to add – sharp kimchi, zingy ginger, salty-savoury soy – you'll know that they'll take that potato fritter in a very interesting direction.

You want it hot enough to colour the potato to a deep golden brown because that adds flavour, but not so hot that the outside is already dark but the inside isn't fully cooked.
A moderate heat and a bit of patience is probably the best way to get this.

If you have a metal ring in this size, this may make it easier.

AMAZAKE DRINK
What is Amazake?

It's a Japanese drink made from fermented rice. It's amazing that amazake isn't better known because not only does it have plenty of health benefits (rich in vitamins and amino acids, good for gut health and metabolism) but it has also been around for more than a millennium in Japan, where it's a traditional part of New Year celebrations and the Doll's Day festival.

The key ingredient is koji, which is in fact a mould (*Aspergillus oryzae*) that is also used to make sake, miso and soy sauce. Added to rice, it causes enzymes to convert carbohydrates into sugars, introducing a lovely delicately sweet taste. In Japan it's sometimes referred to as sweet porridge and I can see why: there's something similarly incredibly warming and comforting about amazake that makes you want to curl up on the sofa in your slippers.

Amazake Drink

120g amazake
200g unsweetened soy milk
50g white chocolate
1 tsp matcha powder
Cricket ketchup (page 309), to taste

Put the amazake and soy milk into a small pan and bring to the boil. Remove the pan from the heat and add the white chocolate and matcha powder. Leave for a minute to allow the chocolate to melt completely into the mixture.

Use a hand blender to blitz the mixture briefly, then strain the mixture through a sieve into a clean pan.

Add a few drops of Cricket ketchup, to taste, and warm through. Blitz the mixture once again, until it's frothy. Serve warm.

A couple of pulses will be enough. You just want to break up the amazake enough to release flavour and some of the body, rather than thoroughly blending it into the drink, which could make the mixture thick and a bit starchy.

It's optional, but I like to add a touch of Cricket ketchup, to introduce some acidity and umami.

HESTON'S SODA BAR
Welcome – what'll you have to drink?

Settle yourself down on a stool at the bar counter and make your choice. Cola? Fanta? Sprite? An ice-cream float? Or something stronger – a beer perhaps?

We can cater for all these tastes. But, this being my soda bar, you won't be surprised to find there's a twist to what I'm serving – namely that the drinks are all made using kombucha, a sweetened fermented tea that has a long tradition in Asian cultures but is only now becoming popular in the West.

The growing interest in kombucha is partly down to health considerations – it contains plenty of vitamins, antioxidants and probiotics that are likely to aid digestion and indeed gut health generally – but it's also testament to the fact that it has a distinctive and delicious flavour: tangy, slightly fizzy, slightly sour, slightly sweet, with some of the characteristics of cider or even ginger ale. It has a unique and complex character that I find very enjoyable.

It's also, as you'll see in the next few pages, highly versatile. You can drink kombucha as is, after the first ferment, or you can add flavourings for the second ferment and take it in a variety of directions.

Kombucha

For the tea stock
1 litre **water**
35g loose-leaf tea (or 12 tea bags) of your choice

For the sugar stock
400g unrefined caster sugar
1 litre **water**

To make the kombucha
3 litres **water**
1 kombucha scoby with strong starter liquid

For the tea stock, bring the **water** to the boil and add the tea. Remove from the heat and leave to infuse for 5 minutes (just 3 minutes for green tea). Strain and set aside to cool.

For the sugar stock, put the sugar and **water** into a pan and place over a medium heat until the sugar is dissolved. Remove from the heat and set aside to cool. You need 1 litre sugar stock.

To make the kombucha, in a large jug or similar container, combine the **water** with the tea stock, sugar stock and kombucha scoby. The mixture should not be too warm.

Pour into a clean 7-litre container (like a large juice dispenser with a tap). Cover with a piece of muslin and secure with an elastic band or string.

Leave to ferment for several days at room temperature and check on the kombucha every second day. It can ferment as quickly as 5 days, but the process can take up to 2 weeks. You will notice it will start to taste pleasantly sour and you can explore for yourself what is the ideal time for you to confirm that it is ready.

Store your kombucha in the fridge – it will keep for a week (if not longer).

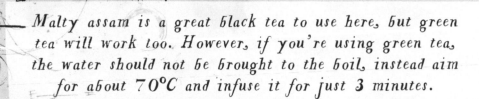

Malty assam is a great black tea to use here, but green tea will work too. However, if you're using green tea, the water should not be brought to the boil, instead aim for about 70°C and infuse it for just 3 minutes.

Kombucha scoby are available online and are essential for kick-starting your own kombucha-making process. The scoby usually arrives stored in a strong starter liquid which should not be discarded.

The scoby (symbiotic culture of bacteria and yeast) is often called the 'mother' because it triggers the whole process, rather like a sourdough 'starter'. It's also sometimes called the 'mushroom' because it can take on that sort of appearance when it forms. Which is a bit sci-fi, but to me this is an exciting transformation - a demonstration of nature at work (as those bacteria and yeasts convert the sugar into ethanol and acetic acid) and a visual sign that flavour and goodness are developing.

If, when you taste, the mixture's still sweet then the kombucha probably needs to be left longer, for the sugars to convert. A slightly sharp, fizzy, cider-like quality is what you're going for. If it's shading into overly sharp or vinegary then it's probably been left to ferment a little too long. As always in cooking, taste, taste, taste.

Lime and Green Peppercorn Kombucha

MAKES ABOUT 810G

1 tsp green peppercorns
Finely pared zest and juice of 2 limes
45g unrefined caster sugar
750g Kombucha (page 290)

Toast the peppercorns in a dry pan over a moderate heat. Set aside a quarter
of the peppercorns (about 10) to use during the fermentation process; lightly
crush the rest of them.

Put the crushed peppercorns into a small pan with the lime zest and juice, and the
sugar. Place over a very low heat to melt the sugar gently. Remove from the heat
and leave to cool and infuse.

Once cooled to room temperature, strain the lime-flavoured syrup and add to
the Kombucha, along with the reserved whole toasted whole peppercorns;
discard the contents of the sieve.

Transfer the mixture to a clean bottle. Leave to ferment for 3 days at room
temperature, opening the bottle every day to allow the mixture to release the gases.

This is best enjoyed chilled, so store in the fridge. It will keep for a week
(if not longer).

Orange and Thyme Kombucha

MAKES ABOUT 850G

200g orange juice (about 2 large oranges)
40g unrefined caster sugar
2–4 sprigs of fresh thyme
750g Kombucha (page 290)

Pour the orange juice into a pan and add the sugar and thyme sprigs. Place
over a moderate heat to dissolve the sugar and then simmer to reduce by half.
Strain the orange syrup into a large bowl and leave to cool.

Once cooled to room temperature, add the Kombucha.

Transfer the mixture to a clean bottle and leave to ferment for 3 days at room
temperature, opening the bottle every day to allow the mixture to release the gases.

This is best enjoyed chilled, so store in the fridge. It will keep for a week
(if not longer).

Kombucha Cola

MAKES ABOUT 900G

For the cola syrup
250g light brown sugar
Pared zest and juice of 7 oranges
Pared zest and juice of 3 lemons
Pared zest and juice of 3 limes
150g molasses
25g coriander seeds
½ nutmeg
20g cola nut powder

To make the cola
750g Kombucha (page 290)
150g Cola syrup (from above)

For the cola syrup, gently melt the sugar in a large non-stick pan to make a dry caramel; do not stir or agitate the sugar. Once completely melted, add all the citrus zests and juice, the molasses and coriander seeds. Grate the nutmeg into the pan too.

Bring to a simmer over a moderate heat and simmer to reduce until you are left with approximately 600g. Stir in the cola nut powder and remove the pan from the heat. Leave to infuse for 15 minutes.

Now strain the syrup through a muslin-lined sieve into a large bowl, squeezing out as much flavour from the citrus zests as possible; discard the contents of the sieve. You should have about 475g syrup. Leave this to cool before using.

To make the cola, in a jug, combine the Kombucha with 150g of the cola syrup (the remaining cola syrup can be reserved for another batch). Transfer the mixture to a clean bottle and leave to ferment for 3 days (see below), opening the bottle every day to allow the mixture to release the gases.

This is best enjoyed chilled, so store in the fridge. It will keep for a week (if not longer).

For more fizz, use an airtight bottle. The pressure will build up as the cola ferments, and the trapped gas will be absorbed into the liquid, creating more bubbles.

Coke Float 'Brown Cow'

MAKES 1

250g Kombucha cola (see opposite), chilled
2 scoops of (R)ice cream (page 327)

This couldn't be easier! Pour the chilled cola in a tall glass and top with a couple of scoops of (R)ice cream... or any ice cream you like, really.

Kombucha Beer

MAKES ABOUT 780G

750g Kombucha (page 290)
50g malt extract
30g unrefined caster sugar
5g hops pellets

Whisk all the ingredients together in a large bowl. Cover and leave to infuse for 6 hours at room temperature.

Strain the mixture into a clean bottle. Leave to ferment for 3 days at room temperature, opening the bottle every day to allow the mixture to release the gases.

This is best enjoyed chilled, so store in the fridge. It will keep for a week (if not longer).

9

Feed the World

How about exploring some alternative edibles?

Cricket Protein Bar

•

Cricket Bread

•

Cricket Ketchup

•

Cricket Biscuits

•

Cricket Stock

•

Take-the-bait Stir-fry

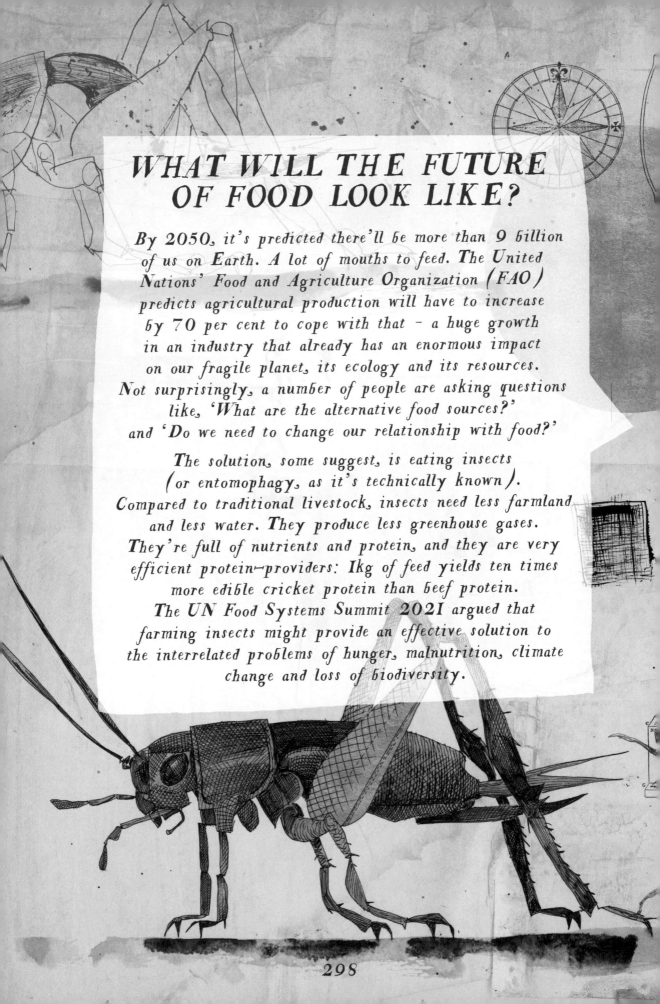

WHAT WILL THE FUTURE OF FOOD LOOK LIKE?

By 2050, it's predicted there'll be more than 9 billion of us on Earth. A lot of mouths to feed. The United Nations' Food and Agriculture Organization (FAO) predicts agricultural production will have to increase by 70 per cent to cope with that – a huge growth in an industry that already has an enormous impact on our fragile planet, its ecology and its resources. Not surprisingly, a number of people are asking questions like, 'What are the alternative food sources?' and 'Do we need to change our relationship with food?'

The solution, some suggest, is eating insects (or entomophagy, as it's technically known). Compared to traditional livestock, insects need less farmland and less water. They produce less greenhouse gases. They're full of nutrients and protein, and they are very efficient protein-providers: 1kg of feed yields ten times more edible cricket protein than beef protein. The UN Food Systems Summit 2021 argued that farming insects might provide an effective solution to the interrelated problems of hunger, malnutrition, climate change and loss of biodiversity.

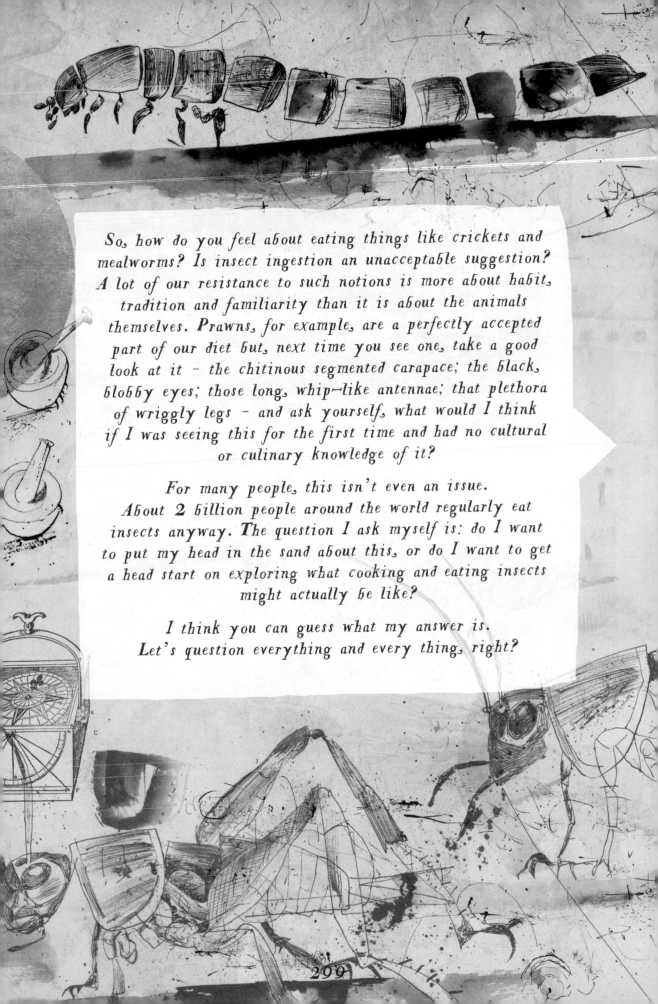

So, how do you feel about eating things like crickets and mealworms? Is insect ingestion an unacceptable suggestion? A lot of our resistance to such notions is more about habit, tradition and familiarity than it is about the animals themselves. Prawns, for example, are a perfectly accepted part of our diet but, next time you see one, take a good look at it – the chitinous segmented carapace; the black, blobby eyes; those long, whip-like antennae; that plethora of wriggly legs – and ask yourself, what would I think if I was seeing this for the first time and had no cultural or culinary knowledge of it?

For many people, this isn't even an issue. About 2 billion people around the world regularly eat insects anyway. The question I ask myself is: do I want to put my head in the sand about this, or do I want to get a head start on exploring what cooking and eating insects might actually be like?

I think you can guess what my answer is. Let's question everything and every thing, right?

CRICKET PROTEIN BAR

What if you could really max out the protein in a protein bar?

I've been exploring the culinary potential of insects for more than a decade, consulting with entomologists like George McGavin to discover the nice (small mealworms) and the definitely not-so-nice (silk moth pupae). For my Victorian Feast programme in 2010 I served guests an edible garden complete with a variety of bugs, and crickets were one of the stars of the show.

Protein-wise, crickets really pack a punch. They're about 65 per cent protein, which is more than beef or chicken. On our increasingly depleted planet, doesn't it seem like a no-brainer to explore this resource? Or is it a step too far?

We might think that our food preferences and taboos are hard-wired but, in fact, many of them grow out of our experiences and associations. They're learned – and can be unlearned. I've found that one way to do this is to take the unfamiliar and house it in a friendly and familiar culinary format. Such as that protein bar we like to munch on-the-go or after an exercise session.

So how about taking the challenge? (Not test cricket but a cricket test.) As you bite into the bar and get those hits of nutty, fruity aromas and encounter interesting textures, you might find the future doesn't look (or taste) so bad.

Cricket Protein Bar

MAKES 8

100g nibbed almonds
150g shelled (hulled) hemp seeds
50g sunflower seeds
50g pumpkin seeds
25g golden linseed
25g chia seeds
150g golden raisins
10g Chinese five-spice powder
30g cricket powder
Finely grated zest of 2 lemons
½ tsp sea salt
180g maple syrup
120g apricot jam
50g chocolate, melted, to finish (optional)

Preheat the oven to 190°C/Fan 170°C/Gas 5. Line a deep-sided tray (about 25 x 18cm) with cling film.

Combine the nibbed almonds with all the seeds and spread out on a large baking tray. Bake for 15–20 minutes, taking the tray out occasionally to stir the mixture to ensure even colouring. Tip the mixture into a bowl and set aside to cool.

Add the raisins, five-spice powder, cricket powder, lemon zest and salt to the toasted seed and nut mix.

Heat the maple syrup and apricot jam together in a medium-small pan, stirring well to combine. Once the mixture reaches a temperature of 125°C, pour it into the bowl of nuts and seeds. Working quickly, mix thoroughly so everything is evenly combined.

Tip the mixture into the lined tray and compress it down to make an even, compact layer. Cover and place in the fridge to cool for at least 2 hours.

Once set, remove from the tray and slice into 8 even-sized bars. Finish with melted chocolate, if you like.

Often people see a list of measured ingredients as a set of instructions, set in stone. But I see it as something else – a springboard for the imagination. An open-ended range of possibilities. An opportunity for exploration. Do you have favourite nuts, seeds or dried fruit? Or favourite combos? Add them in. If there are ones you don't like, just take them out. A recipe is yours to take ownership of. Explore it. Try it this way and that until you've personalised it.

There's an incredible burst of aromas when you add the five-spice and the lemon to the mix. That bright, sharp freshness of citrus. The fragrant, warming zing of ground star anise, fennel seed, peppercorn, clove, cinnamon. You get a real sense of how some ingredients really punch above their weight and can bring a recipe alive.

A jam thermometer or digital probe is essential here to check the temperature of the syrup.

Do you want to top with a little chocolate? Then gently melt some in a small pan and drizzle over the bars, or dip them in it.

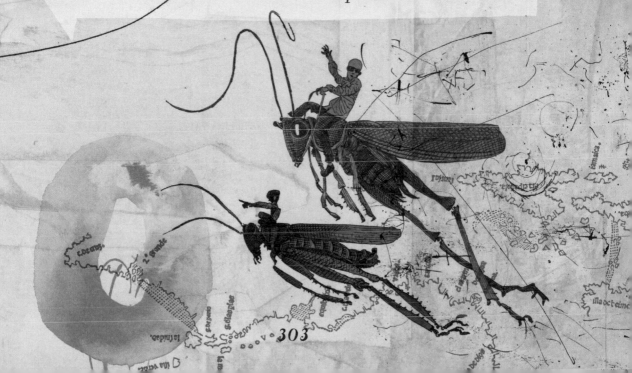

CRICKET BREAD
Something to prove?

Bread-making is perhaps one of the most accessible ways to explore this new and unfamiliar ingredient. You'll end up with a lovely focaccia-style loaf, with the cricket powder bringing plenty of extra savoury flavour.

Cricket Bread

400g tepid water
2 tsp active dried yeast (7g)
Pinch of unrefined caster sugar
25g olive oil, plus an extra 20g oil to brush
420g strong white bread flour
80g cricket powder
2 tsp fine salt
Sea salt flakes

Combine the water, yeast and sugar in a bowl and set aside for 10 minutes to activate the yeast, then whisk in the olive oil.

Put the flour, cricket powder and salt into a stand mixer fitted with the dough hook attachment. With the mixer on a low speed setting, slowly pour in the yeast mixture over a 10-minute period until the mixture comes together as a loose ball of dough.

Transfer the dough to a bowl, cover with oiled cling film and leave to rise for 1 hour at room temperature.

Place the loose ball of dough on a clean surface and use a pastry scraper to turn it in on itself 3–5 times to build the gluten strength. Return it to the bowl and leave for another 30 minutes, covered with oiled cling film. Repeat this kneading and resting process.

Line a baking tray, about 20 x 25cm, with lightly oiled baking paper.

Repeat the kneading process once more, then transfer the dough to the prepared tray. Brush the surface with just a little olive oil and leave to prove at room temperature for 45 minutes this time.

In the meantime, preheat the oven to 220°C/Fan 200°C/Gas 7.

When ready to bake, flatten the dough, spreading it out into the corners of the tray. Use oiled fingers to make indentations all over the surface of the dough to create a dimpled effect. Brush with the rest of the olive oil and scatter over the sea salt flakes. Bake for 30 minutes.
Cool on a wire rack.

Check the labelling on the packet: the flour must contain at least 13 per cent protein to achieve the desired bread texture.

This might seem a lengthy and repetitive process, but it is going to help activate the yeast, fold in oxygen and create lots of bubbles in the dough.

'And lots of bubbles means lighter bread with a finer crumb!'

The bread will tell you when it's nearing readiness by releasing that fantastic toasty aroma. You'll see a crust has formed and the loaf has begun to shrink and move away a little from the tray's edges.

CRICKET KETCHUP

Can you really have a ketchup without tomato?

Dutch traders introduced kêtsiap, a Chinese fermented fish sauce, to Europe around 1700. Although we now think of it as a tomato-based condiment, early British versions generally used mushrooms but also experimented with many other ingredients – oysters, mussels, walnuts, anchovies, beer, elderberries, cucumbers.

So why not revive that tradition, I thought, and introduce cricket powder to the mix? The result is a condiment with a nice spicy, savoury sourness that you can stash in the fridge and use in much the same way as you would Worcestershire sauce, to add a bit of pep to a dish.

Cricket Ketchup

500g **water**
1 star anise
½ cinnamon stick
1 clove
100g cricket powder
20g unrefined golden caster sugar
1 tsp malt vinegar
½ tsp salt

Put the **water**, star anise, cinnamon and clove into a pan and bring to the boil.
Remove from the heat.

Stir in the cricket powder. Leave to infuse for 5 minutes.

Pass the infused liquid through a coffee filter into a bowl, discarding the sludgy
pulp in the filter.

Stir in the sugar, vinegar and salt. Taste the ketchup for seasoning and add a little
more salt and/or vinegar if required.

Store in a sealed, clean bottle or jar in the fridge and use within a week.

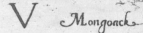

Smell the liquid at this stage and what do you get
– a five-spicy, almost Christmassy aroma?

And smell it now. Has it changed and developed?

Cricket powder is extremely fine, so you need a finer
mesh than a sieve or muslin cloth to strain it.
A coffee filter provides a simple but effective solution.

Ketchup's a go-to for burgers and/or chips, but it's
way more versatile than that, so why not catch up with
ketchup's other possibilities? Add some to stews and
curries and suchlike for a hit of richness and sweetness.
Or to tomato sauces – for pasta, for barbecues – for that
sweet-sour kick. You could freeze the ketchup in an
ice-cube tray so you've always got some to hand.

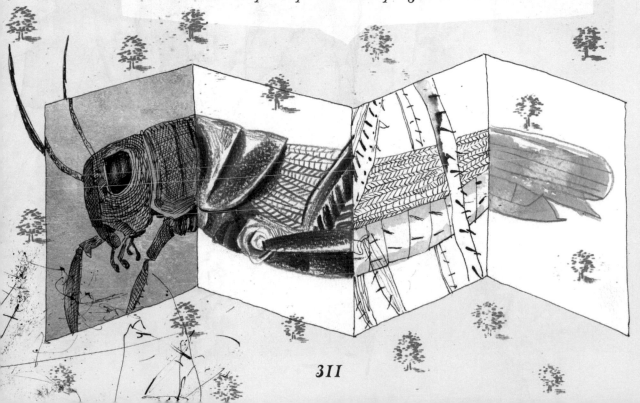

CRICKET BISCUITS

What's my best way into cooking with crickets?

It's probably these biscuits. After all, who doesn't love a biscuit? Plus, the flavour's not too strong and the mixture combines well with chocolate to create a tasty little nibble that also gives you a shot of protein. And how many biscuits can claim that?

Cricket Biscuits

MAKES 16–18

250g unsalted butter, softened
125g unrefined golden caster sugar
1 large egg
1 large egg yolk
40g cocoa powder
50g cricket powder
200g plain flour, sifted
70g chocolate chips
20g whole milk

Using a stand mixer fitted with the paddle attachment, cream together the butter and sugar until pale and smooth. Add the whole egg and extra yolk and mix until incorporated.

Now add the cocoa powder, cricket powder and flour to the mixture, and mix on a low speed until evenly combined. Lastly add the chocolate chips and milk and mix briefly until incorporated.

Tip the mixture onto a sheet of cling film and roll into a log, about 6cm in diameter. Wrap the log in the cling film, sealing the ends, and place in the fridge to set for several hours, preferably overnight.

When ready to bake, preheat the oven to 180°C/Fan 160°C/Gas 4 and line a large baking tray with baking paper.

Unwrap the log and slice into 16–18 discs, about 1cm thick. Place the dough rounds on the prepared tray, leaving a little space in between as they will spread a little. (You may need to bake the biscuits in batches, depending on the size of your tray.)

Place the tray on the middle shelf of the oven and bake for 11 minutes. Transfer the biscuits to a wire rack to cool.

How many of our food taboos are preconceptions or learned opinions? We can all be a bit nervous with a new ingredient but, in the end, once you get into the rhythms of baking and the pleasures of preparation, isn't it just another powder to add?

After childhood, it's not often we get to taste a brand new, never-before-encountered ingredient. Why not have a first nibble with that in mind – has it taken that choc-chip bikkie in a different direction? Is there a slight savouriness to complement the other ingredients?

'Like my cricket protein bars on page 301, these biscuits are bursting with protein. So why not put aside those protein shakes and bake a batch of these instead to use as your post-workout energy boost?'

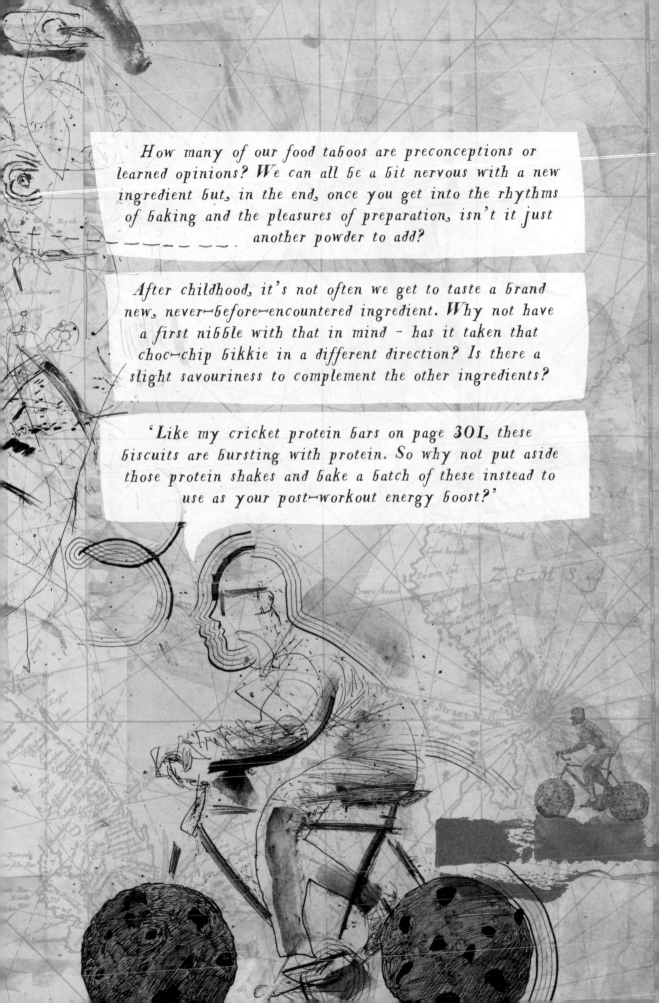

CRICKET STOCK

What if you could make a powerfully savoury stock with a tiny handful of ingredients?

What can I say? Try this and I guarantee that you'll be amazed at the depth of flavour you get in such a short time using just three ingredients.

'Waiter, there's a cricket in my soup.'

Cricket Stock

MAKES 1 LITRE

2 litres **water**
400g cricket powder
Salt, to taste

Bring the **water** to the boil in a pan. Add the cricket powder and remove from the heat. Leave the mixture to infuse for 5 minutes only.

Strain the stock through a coffee filter into a bowl, discarding the pulpy sludge. Season with salt to taste. Leave to cool unless using straight away.

Store, covered, in the fridge and use within 5 days.

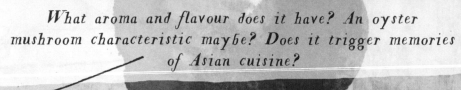

What aroma and flavour does it have? An oyster mushroom characteristic maybe? Does it trigger memories of Asian cuisine?

I wonder how this would work with a boost of umami. You could try adding a strip of kombu to the filtered liquid and letting it infuse for an hour to see if that adds an extra dimension.

This stock is showcased in the delicious Cricket pho on page 107. But you could also use it in any dish in place of chicken stock.

fig.9

TAKE–THE–BAIT STIR–FRY

Have you ever eaten an insect?

Inevitably, I've had to eat lots. Partly because I'm unstoppably curious about food, cooking and ingredients and I question everything, and I don't really believe in food taboos. Partly, too, because when I make TV programmes, the directors love to strong–arm me into eating oddities on film. (Eventually I made a pact: I'd continue to do so, but only if they ate the end result as well. Unsurprisingly, there were subsequently fewer requests for me to eat leeches or gobble grasshoppers.)

During my ongoing investigation of edible insects, one of the tastiest I've come across are mealworms, which in fact aren't a worm at all, they're the larvae of a beetle and they have a lovely nutty flavour. They're also not too fatty and a good source of vitamins, fibre and protein. I served them up once as a pizza topping to kids at the Alder Hey Children's Hospital and they gave it the thumbs up.

So why not give them a try in this stir–fry of spicy fish and mealworms?

321

Take-the-bait Stir-fry

SERVES 2

For the ginger chilli paste
2 shallots, peeled and roughly chopped
2 red chillies, roughly chopped
2 garlic cloves, peeled and roughly chopped
40g peeled and roughly chopped fresh ginger
6 tbsp **water**
1 tbsp kecap manis

For the stir-fry
15g small mealworms (about 4 tbsp)
300g monkfish tail
2 heads of pak choi
175g baby corn
1 tsp sesame oil
1 tsp vegetable oil
3 tbsp **water**
2 handfuls of bean sprouts
2 tbsp Japanese special sauce 'umamilicious' (page 251)
Small handful of fresh coriander
2 spring onions, finely sliced
Finely grated zest of 1 lime, saving the wedges to serve

For the ginger chilli paste, use a hand blender or mini food chopper to blitz all the ingredients to a paste. Set aside.

Heat a frying pan over a high heat, add the mealworms and cook until toasted and crispy. Remove from the pan and set aside.

To prepare the fish and veg, cut the monkfish into smaller pieces, about 25g each. Slice each pak choi lengthways into 8 wedges (through the core so each wedge holds together). Slice each baby corn lengthways into 4 even pieces.

Add the sesame oil and vegetable oil to a wok or large non-stick sauté pan over a medium-high heat. Carefully add the fish pieces, cooking them on one side only. Remove from the pan and set aside.

Add the ginger chilli paste, corn, pak choi and **water** to the pan and cook for about 2 minutes over a medium-high heat, shaking the pan regularly to ensure even cooking.

Return the fish to the pan and add the bean sprouts. Take the pan off the heat and stir through the Japanese special sauce.

Divide the stir-fry between 2 warmed bowls. Finely chop the coriander and scatter over the stir-fry, along with the sliced spring onions and lime zest.

Just before serving, sprinkle over the crunchy mealworms. Serve with lime wedges for squeezing.

Get hold of small mealworms rather than large,
as these are far tastier.

Are you getting a delicious nutty aroma from the pan?

You need to get these ready in advance because, once the
pan's on the heat, there's no stopping with a stir-fry.

Now we're in familiar territory – channelling the
street-food vibe, quick-frying ingredients,
enjoying the heat and steam and sizzle and clouds
of aroma as we flip 'n' stir. Stir-frying's such
an energetic, aromatic, full-on fun bit of cooking.

This stir-fry has an incredible flavour complexity
from all those punchy ingredients, which is given a boost
by this truly umamilicious sauce.

'Fish and their bait
in the same dish.
See what you did there, boss.
You sure do love a visual
culinary pun.'

10

Just Desserts

Fancy something sweet?

(R)ice Cream

•

Tarte Tatin

•

Hemp Panna Cotta

•

Double-baked Cookies

•

Sherry Vinegar Posset

•

Quantum Pastilles

(R)ICE CREAM

What if I could make breakfast into a dessert?

It might seem like an unlikely question.
(Though, in truth, that's my favourite kind, as they're
the ones that take me on the most interesting journeys.)
And like an unlikely source of inspiration.
But that's where this dish starts.

Back in the 1990s at The Fat Duck I was cooking
parsnips for a purée to accompany sweetbreads, and when
I tasted the milk they'd been poached in, it was a
deeply nostalgic experience. It had a flavour that
took me straight back to childhood and the milk at the
bottom of the cereal bowl. So I began developing a
parsnip cereal as part of a breakfast-as-dessert dish.

(R)ice Cream

MAKES ABOUT 1.1KG

375g basmati rice
300g Rice Krispies
1.5 litres unsweetened rice milk
60g coconut oil
150g inulin prebiotic powder
150g rice syrup
150g crème fraîche

Preheat the oven to 250°C/Fan 230°C/Gas 10.

Spread the rice out on a large baking tray and toast in the oven for
8–15 minutes until golden, stirring every 5 minutes and rotating the tray
to ensure even toasting.

Combine the Rice Krispies and rice milk in a large bowl and set aside
to infuse for 5–6 minutes, gently stirring the mixture every now and then
to ensure maximum infusion.

Strain the mixture into a clean bowl; the infused milk yield should
be approximately 900g.

Add the toasted basmati rice to the infused milk. Cover and leave in the
fridge overnight, but no longer than 12 hours.

Strain into a pan; the yield should be approximately 700g. Bring to a light simmer,
adding the coconut oil, inulin and rice syrup.

Use a hand blender to blitz well, ensuring the coconut oil is emulsified into the
warm milk and the inulin has completely dissolved. Leave to cool in the fridge
for 2–3 hours.

Once chilled, add the crème fraîche and blitz a second time, then pour into your
ice-cream maker and churn according to the manufacturer's instructions.

After churning, remove the mixture and blitz with a hand blender for
10 seconds, then return to the machine to churn for another 10 minutes.

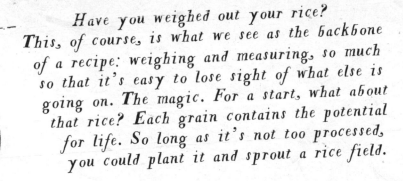

Have you weighed out your rice?
This, of course, is what we see as the backbone
of a recipe: weighing and measuring, so much
so that it's easy to lose sight of what else is
going on. The magic. For a start, what about
that rice? Each grain contains the potential
for life. So long as it's not too processed,
you could plant it and sprout a rice field.

Just pouring rice onto a baking tray starts to stir
my emotions – the trickle of grains through the fingers,
the pattering sound as they hit the tray like raindrops.
Then there's the smell of the rice as it begins to cook.
Don't you find there's a kind of comforting warmth
to that aroma? Like bread baking. Or coffee brewing.

This has got to be
one of the pleasures of cooking,
that sensory richness that happens
when we let go for a moment
from the concerns of timings
and temperatures
and measurements.

Did you eat Rice Krispies as a
kid? This is where I can get completely
drawn into the memories and emotions.
    For a while I forgot I had a recipe
to finish and felt as though I was sinking
into the bowl, listening to that snap,
crackle and pop.

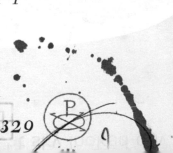

TARTE TATIN

Why are you eating your apple tart upside down?

Legend has it that the Tatin sisters messed up the prep of their apple tart and figured the best way to fix it was to put the pastry on top, pop it in the oven anyway, and then flip it over before serving. The result of this 'mistake' was a dessert full of rich, sticky, buttery, golden-brown caramelised deliciousness.

Whether or not this story is true (an upside-down fruit tart was already a speciality of the Sologne region in France), it still serves as a reminder that there's not necessarily one way or the 'right' way of doing things in the kitchen, and that we shouldn't fear getting things wrong.
Just get in the kitchen and have a go.

Tarte Tatin

SERVES 4

80g unsalted butter, softened
100g unrefined caster sugar
1 star anise
5–6 Granny Smith apples
1 sheet ready-rolled puff pastry (all-butter, if possible)
Plain flour, for dusting

Spread the softened butter evenly over the bottom of a pan suitable for use on the hob and in the oven, about 20cm in diameter. Sprinkle over the sugar and add the star anise.

Peel and halve the apples, removing the cores. Cut each apple half in two. Pack the apple wedges side by side in the pan, pointing upwards.

Place the pan over a medium heat to melt the butter and dissolve the sugar. Cook until the mixture is bubbling and turns light golden. Remove the pan from the heat and set aside to cool completely.

Preheat the oven to 200°C/Fan 180°C/Gas 6.

Roll out the puff pastry sheet on a lightly floured work surface to a 2–3mm thickness and cut out a disc, 1cm larger all round than your pan.

Once the apples have cooled, roll the pastry around your rolling pin, place over the pan and unroll it over the apples. Carefully tuck the pastry in around the edges of the tin, under the apples, and make several holes in the top with a small knife.

Bake for 35 minutes or until the pastry is a light golden brown. Remove from the oven and turn the Tatin out while it is still warm, else it may stick to the pan. Pick out and discard the star anise.

Serve the Tarte Tatin warm, with cream, ice cream or even custard.

This recipe's a showcase for those beautifully browned apples rather than the pastry. So, I'd definitely use store-bought puff, which makes the dish very simple to prepare, without compromising on flavour or texture.

A pan with a heavy base is your friend for this recipe, as it's less likely to have hot spots where the caramel might burn.

Sometimes I add a few lightly roasted hazelnuts to the pan before topping with the pastry. A bit of extra texture and flavour... and toasty-ness.

Get a plate large enough to hold the tart. Place it, upside-down, on top of the pan. Steady your hands. Deep breath. Carefully flip the pan over. Maybe give it a gentle shake. You should hear a schlooompf as the tart slides from pan to plate.

HEMP PANNA COTTA

Isn't it all about the wobble?

For me, some dishes are about getting that just–set texture. When you shake the plate and something gives, that little quiver tells you it's going to be soft and melting in the mouth. Panna cotta is one of these. It's not the end of the world if it ends up firm (it's happened to all of us), but the real majesty of a panna cotta is its delicate texture. And there's a real sense of achievement when you pull that off. If food is about emotion, then that pride and satisfaction is just going to make the panna cotta taste even better.

Hemp Panna Cotta

For the panna cotta
380g unsweetened hemp milk
190g double cream
50g honey
6g gelatine powder

For the rhubarb compote
125g rhubarb; 75g roughly chopped and 50g thinly sliced
15g unrefined caster sugar
25g water

For the crumble
25g unsalted butter, finely diced
30g plain flour
1 tbsp unrefined caster sugar
20g shelled (hulled) hemp seeds
Pinch of salt

For the panna cotta, bring the hemp milk to a simmer in a pan and simmer until reduced by half (to about 190g). Add the cream and honey to the pan and gently warm through over a medium heat. Add the gelatine and stir well until it is completely dissolved; do not allow the mixture to come to the boil. Strain the mixture to ensure there are no undissolved pieces of gelatine.

Now pour the mixture equally into 4 ramekins or small bowls (approximately 105g in each). Cover and leave to set in the fridge for at least 4 hours.

To make the compote, put the chopped rhubarb into a small pan with the sugar and **water**. Cook over a medium-low heat for about 10 minutes until the mixture is reduced by half and the rhubarb has cooked down to a purée. Add the sliced rhubarb and cook for a further 3 minutes until softened. Set aside to cool, then cover and place in the fridge.

For the crumble, preheat the oven to 180°C/Fan 160°C/Gas 4. Combine the butter, flour, sugar, shelled hemp seeds and salt in a bowl. Using your fingertips, rub the mixture together until it resembles coarse breadcrumbs.

Spread the mixture out evenly on a baking tray and bake for about 15–20 minutes until golden, checking every 5 minutes and stirring it around with a fork to prevent clumping and ensure even colouring. Remove from the oven and leave to cool.

To turn out the panna cottas, fill a small bowl with warm **water**. One at a time, lower each ramekin into the **water** for 10 seconds, then remove and invert a little serving plate on top of the ramekin. Turn the plate and mould upside down to allow the panna cotta to gently tip out onto the plate.

Spoon the rhubarb compote on top of the hemp panna cottas and surround with the crumble.

'For me, hemp milk really suits a panna cotta, introducing a delicate but distinctive strand of savouriness that lifts it above the blandly neutral. I wonder what other plant-based milks might bring to the dish. You could try an almond one, for example, and accentuate it by using ground almonds in the crumble.'

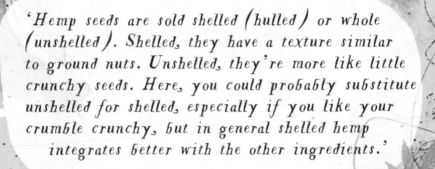

'Hemp seeds are sold shelled (hulled) or whole (unshelled). Shelled, they have a texture similar to ground nuts. Unshelled, they're more like little crunchy seeds. Here, you could probably substitute unshelled for shelled, especially if you like your crumble crunchy, but in general shelled hemp integrates better with the other ingredients.'

'A lot of people are daunted by the challenge of setting an ingredient, but the key to it is straightforward. Each one of those granules of gelatine makes a contribution to the thickening so you want to make sure as many as possible are dissolved into the liquid.'

'The other key thing to remember is that, while some like it hot, gelatine doesn't. So, it's worth keeping an eye on the warming panna cotta mixture and taking it off the heat as soon as the first bubbles appear.'

DOUBLE-BAKED COOKIES

As a kid, did you use to eat those bits of biscuit at the bottom of the biscuit tin?

The original inspiration for these cookies was a nostalgic chat me and my development team had about the biscuity rubble you find in a biscuit tin, which warped into wondering if there was some way we could use them in a dish. I was influenced too by a bit of culinary wordplay: the word 'biscuit' comes from the French – bis cuit – which means twice-cooked (because that's how they were made in the past, either by cooking and drying in a low oven or by boiling then frying). Most biscuits are not cooked twice any more, so it tickled my imagination to give the biscuit back its historical heritage.

So why not take those biscuity bits and cook them into cookies?

1576

Double-baked Cookies

MAKES 8

For the cookie dough base
300g old biscuits, crushed to a crumb
80g melted unsalted butter
1 ripe banana, mashed

For the caramel brittle
100g unrefined caster sugar
35g unsalted butter

For the chocolate and caramel cookies
30g chopped dark chocolate
30g Caramel brittle (from above)

For the orange and sour cherry cookies
Finely grated zest of 1 orange
30g sour cherries (or dried cranberries)

Combine the crushed biscuits, melted butter and mashed banana in a bowl until the mixture comes together as a dough. Divide into two equal portions (about 240g each) and set aside.

To make the caramel brittle, melt the sugar in a heavy-based pan over a medium heat, without stirring or agitating it.

In the meantime, line a tray with baking paper. When the sugar is completely melted and turned golden, add the butter and stir until fully incorporated. Pour the caramel onto the lined tray in a thin layer and leave to cool and set completely. Once cold, break the caramel brittle up into smaller pieces.

To bake the cookies, preheat the oven to 200°C/Fan 180°C/Gas 6 and line a large baking tray with baking paper.

For the chocolate and caramel cookies, mix the chopped chocolate and caramel brittle into one portion of dough, shape into 4 balls and place on one half of the prepared tray.

For the orange and sour cherry cookies, mix the orange zest and sour cherries into the other portion of dough and shape into 4 balls. Place on the other half of the prepared tray.

Press the balls down to flatten into rounds and bake for 10–15 minutes until golden.

Leave the cookies on the tray to firm up for a few minutes then transfer to a wire rack to cool.

You can use any old biscuits or biscuit crumbs for this recipe, but it's best if they don't have a filling. Digestive biscuits and Hobnobs work really well.

'I've given two cookie flavours here: chocolate and caramel, and orange and sour cherry. If you'd prefer to make only one of the two flavours, simply double up the ingredients listed for the one you choose, and use to flavour the full batch of cookie dough.'

It's always a good idea to rotate the tray halfway through to ensure even baking.

They'll firm up somewhat as they cool so don't worry if the texture's not yet quite cookie-like when they exit the oven.

SHERRY VINEGAR POSSET

Vinegar...in a dessert!?

Sherry vinegar's not just for vinaigrettes. I put it in all sorts of dishes, including the Egg and rocket sandwich on page 45, the tomato compote on page 174 and in the mushroom purée for the Sunshine in a bowl soup on page 97. I've used it too in scrambled eggs, spag bol and potted Stilton. Why?

Because it's not too acidic, not too sweet and has a complex nutty flavour, which means it's a great way to add complexity to a dish or counterbalance the richness of the other ingredients. Sometimes it's just a seasoning. Other times, it can be one of the stars of the show, as here.

As well as introducing flavour, the sherry helps create the thickened texture of this dish. A posset is basically cream that has curdled because acid has been added, which makes its casein proteins cluster into clumps, causing it to set. Traditionally, lemon was used for this, but the acid in vinegar works just as well and brings that lovely nuttiness to the party.

343

Sherry Vinegar Posset

MAKES 4

For the prune compote
80g pitted dried prunes
1 Earl Grey tea bag (or 2g loose leaves secured in a muslin parcel)
3g finely pared lemon zest
1 star anise
10g unrefined golden caster sugar
100g boiling **water**

For the posset
35g sherry vinegar
250g double cream
65g honey

To finish
20g toasted nuts of your choice

Place the prunes, tea bag, lemon zest, star anise and sugar in a bowl.
Pour on the boiling hot **water** to cover and leave to macerate for 24 hours
at room temperature.

The next day, pick out and discard the tea bag, lemon zest and star anise.
Set the prune compote aside.

For the posset, bring the sherry vinegar to the boil in a very small pan and
simmer until it is reduced by half (to little more than 1 tbsp).

In a separate pan, gently warm the cream over a medium-low heat. Add the
honey and reduced sherry vinegar, mixing well to combine. Remove from the
heat and pour into 4 small ramekins. Place in the fridge for at least 3 hours to set.

Serve the sherry vinegar posset with the prune compote spooned over. Just before
tucking in, mix the whole lot together and scatter over toasted nuts of your choice.

This is a flavourful set of ingredients. Pick out a prune and have a taste. Maybe try a little sip of sherry vinegar alongside. Don't you think that rich, dark fruitiness will pick up and complement the vinegar's characteristics?

What about the other aromatics you'll be infusing overnight? That fresh citrus zing. The fruity, almost perfumed, fragrance of Earl Grey. The warm woody spiciness of the star anise. Already, once you pour on the water, aromas will arise and make themselves known.

Have a little sip of the mixture now and then smell it after a few hours. The aroma will have evolved, as the tea notes come through and the ingredients intermingle. This is flavour-building at work.

There's a beauty and a pleasure in something so simple. And it gives me a kick that I'm making something that has a real link to the past. The dish dates back to at least the fifteenth century and makes an appearance in three of Shakespeare's plays. This is for me part of the power and emotional value of cooking: the way in which it can connect us all, across centuries and generations.

Pine nuts are great in this dish, but any nuts will work. To toast pine nuts, spread them out in a small tray and bake in an oven preheated to 200°C/Fan 180°C/Gas 6 for 7-8 minutes until golden. Keep your eyes (and nose) on them and you'll know when they're ready.

QUANTUM PASTILLES
IF EVERYTHING ISN'T QUANTUM, WHAT IS IT?

Looking back, I realise I always had what I now think of as a quantum perspective on gastronomy. I just didn't know to call it that.

I've always been fascinated by how our experience of food and flavour is influenced by our expectations, by what perspective we choose to take, and I've constantly been creating dishes that reflect that fascination.

These pastilles have their origin in my search, about **20** years ago, for suitable veg for savoury pâte de fruits. I settled on beetroot but struggled with setting it to the texture I wanted, so I kept increasing the acidity until a funny thing happened. Beetroot became blackcurrant. Or so it seemed. It was so uncanny I began serving it at the restaurant as a red pastille. One woman put it in her mouth then asked the waiter:

'What is this?'

'Madame, it's b...'

'...eetroot? I don't like beetroot!'

'...lackcurrant.'

'Lovely. I wouldn't eat it if it were beetroot.'

That's the quantum perspective right there. Is the pastille beetroot or blackcurrant? We taste things all the time and let our mouth and nose judge what we are putting in our mouths. It's a question of perspective.

347

Quantum Pastilles

510g vegetable juice of your choice
100g glucose syrup
13g tartaric acid
350g unrefined caster sugar
12g yellow pectin (see below)
Granulated sugar, to coat

Pour 500g of your vegetable juice into a pan and add the glucose syrup over a high heat. While you are waiting for it to come to a boil, combine the remaining 10g vegetable juice with the tartaric acid in a small bowl. In a separate small bowl, mix together the caster sugar and pectin.

When the mixture is boiling, scatter the sugar/pectin mix into the pan and keep an eye on the temperature you are aiming for, which is 108°C. This can take approximately 30 minutes. If you have a refractometer, aim for 69°Bx.

Once at temperature, stir in the tartaric acid mixture and remove from the heat.

Carefully pour the mix into pastille moulds and leave to set at room temperature for at least 12 hours.

Once set, carefully remove the pastilles and roll them in granulated sugar until coated on all sides.

It's very important to use yellow pectin (also called pectine jaune) to make these pastilles, not regular pectin powder. Alternatively, you could use 360g jam sugar (with added pectin) instead of the caster sugar and pectin mixture.

You can use any vegetable, but beetroot, butternut squash and Romano peppers work well because they flip convincingly to blackcurrant, apricot and rhubarb respectively.
You'll probably need to juice about 1.2kg fresh, peeled vegetables to yield 510g juice.

The beetroot pastille, then, is a perfect symbol of what quantum gastronomy is all about. I was so excited by this that last year I began serving these and other flavour-flips at The Fat Duck as part of the final 'Like a Kid in a Sweetshop' course, packaged in a foil-and-paper tube as a nostalgic nod to sweets of my youth.

Why not try them and see what you think?

What's Cooking?

As we all know, water is life. It makes up about 60 per cent of our bodies. Without it, we can only survive a few days. It's fundamental to our existence. Did you notice, in this book, how often water is a key part of the cooking process – as a cooking medium or as an ingredient in its own right? Not forgetting how much is present in other ingredients. (That seemingly solid potato is, in fact, around 80 per cent water.)

Colourless, odourless, it seems such a simple thing and we tend to take it for granted. But water is, in fact, a mystery that defies the laws of physics.

Water expands and becomes less dense when it turns into a solid, which means that – unlike almost all other substances – its solid form floats on its liquid form. It has the strength to break apart rocks and help plants push through concrete. It has an unusually high melting point, boiling point and surface tension. It can move against gravity. It freezes faster when it's hot. And that's just the beginning. Water has more than 50 properties that it shares with almost no other liquids. Some scientists are now even suggesting that water has memory. Or that it is in fact composed of two co-existing liquid structures.

Simple or complex? One liquid or two? Water is a great example of the point I've been trying to make in this book: there's always more than one perspective. Everything is quantum.

Given how essential water is to our cooking, it makes sense to me to explore it from every perspective. Some researchers suggest water carries energy, or that it can be changed by crystals or sound or electro-magnetic fields. Are they right? I don't know, and many people dismiss such ideas out of hand.

But history is full of people who were originally doubted but later vindicated. Galileo was convicted of heresy and put under house arrest for promoting Copernicus's theory that the Earth goes round the sun. Van Gogh sold almost none of his paintings during his lifetime, but his canvases now change hands for more than $100 million. If pioneering scientists turn out to be right about some of these suggested characteristics of water, think how exciting that might be for cooking, and what possibilities it might open up.

For each of us, what we cook and how we cook depends on our perspective. For me, it's all about keeping an open mind and nurturing the imagination. Question everything – that's my approach to cooking. What's yours…

vegetable and guacamole
tacos 164–5
take-the-bait stir-fry 321–3
tamari
hemp satay 266–7
Japanese special sauce
'umamilicious' 252–3
tarragon
exhilarating green gazpacho
89–91
herb dressing 148
refried beans 162
tartare sauce 220
tarte Tatin 331–3
tastes 202, 251
tea
kombucha 290–1
prune compote 344–5
teff 265
tempeh 265
with hemp satay 267
Texas 231
thermometers, digital probe 243
thyme
comforting braised beef soup
104–5
creamy tomato soup 118–9
orange and thyme kombucha
292
tikka kebab, chicken 186–7
toast
bacon butty 25–7
bone marrow toast 104–5
kimcheese toastie 33–5
toasting nuts 95, 143, 345
tofu
kimchi miso dressing 270–1
tomato ketchup 251
bacon butty 26–7
Marie Rose sauce 42–3
Moroccan pasties 168–71
steak butter 162–3
tomato compote ketchup
261–3
tomatoes
barbecue vegetable salad
130–1
chilli con carne with spiced
chocolate 232–5
creamy tomato soup 117–19
exhilarating green gazpacho
89–91
invigorating strawberry and
tomato soup 93–5
lamb curry 188–9
a macerated salad 127
pan bagnat 50–1

pasta puttanesca 180–1
pico de gallo 160–1
prawn cocktail salad
sandwich 42–3
quinoa with vegetables 138–9
ratatouille 174–7
semi-dried tomatoes 138
tomato and coffee muffins
65–7
tomato compote 174–7
tonka beans 97
tortillas 157–9
see also tacos
triple cooked chips 212–13
tuna
pan bagnat 50–1
tzatziki 255

U

umami 119, 251
United Nations Food Systems
Summit (2021) 298

V

Van Gogh, Vincent 352
vanilla
Marie Rose sauce 42_3
vegetables
caramelising 243
quantum pastilles 347–9
vegetable and guacamole
tacos 164–5
see also carrots, peppers,
salads etc
Vietnam 107
vinaigrette 122–3, 145–7
Asian-style vinaigrette 147
a macerated salad 127
mustard vinaigrette 146
shallot and caper vinaigrette
146
vinegar
beetroot and pea salad 134–5
'boiled' dressing 149
classic vinaigrette 146
gut-friendly beetroot soup
112–14
hedgerow salad 142–3
pickled beetroot 112, 142
pickled fennel seeds 210–11
pickled onions 164
poached eggs 71
sherry vinegar 181
sherry vinegar posset 343–5
vegetable and guacamole
tacos 164–5

vinaigrette 145–7
with fish and chips 211
vitamin D 97

W

Wales, fish and chips 211
water 11, 352
watercress 45, 143
exhilarating green gazpacho
89–91
Waterside Inn, Bray 261
wheat 198–9
wild garlic 143
wine
chilli con carne with spiced
chocolate 232–5
comforting braised beef soup
103–5
wine vinegar
beetroot and pea salad 134–5
'boiled' dressing 149
classic vinaigrette 146
gut-friendly beetroot soup
112–14
hedgerow salad 142–3
pickled fennel seeds 210–11
vegetable and guacamole
tacos 164–5

Y

yeasts 291
cricket bread 306–7
yoghurt
aubergine and spinach biryani
192–5
bacon and egg porridge 84–5
chicken tikka kebab 186–7
extra-thick yoghurt 259
herb dressing 148
lamb curry 188–9
naan 196–9
raitziki 255–9
yoghurt dressing 147
Yorkshire puddings 246–7

With characteristic intellectual energy, diplomacy and good humour, my Chief Marketing Officer, James Winter, kept this show somehow on the road, even when the going was tough. But for him, this book would never have made the finishing line and I'm in his debt. As I am to my CEO, Richard Turnbull, who has been the perfect guiding light for this project – wise, patient and quietly supportive.

Mention should be made, too, of Otto Romer, who got this book going in the first place, with his usual care, consideration and inventiveness. My development chefs, Ashley Hatton and Deiniol Pritchard, assisted by Belen Aloisi, Eduardo Brambilla, Loris Caporizzi, Ewoud Dudok de Wit, Francisco Castro Fernandes and my son, Jack, did an extraordinary job of taking my ideas, exploring their possibilities and putting up with my refinements until we had a wonderful set of recipes. Their enthusiasm and creativity are at the heart of this book. As is the imagination, organisation and determination of Monya Kilian Palmer, who was my project manager for the book and threw everything at it, including the kitchen sink (because she also worked on recipe development).

For the words themselves, I have to acknowledge the contribution of Pascal Cariss, who's worked with me for the last fifteen years and developed an uncanny ability to take in my ideas, notes, writings and comments and turn them into a better version of themselves. It's a good partnership.

At Bloomsbury my commissioning editor, Rowan Yapp, has been everything you could hope for in an editor: receptive, creative, calm, enthusiastic and seemingly unruffled by any curve ball sent her way. (There were a lot.) Similarly, in-house project editor Lena Hall really 'got' this project and confidently guided it forwards, while offering lots of invaluable suggestions. The production controller, Laura Brodie, did an amazing and meticulous job of turning all the ideas, words and visuals into an actual physical book that looks as good as I'd hoped. And, through their outstanding media savvy and resourcefulness, publicity manager Philippa Cotton and marketing manager Beth Maher did an equally great job at bringing this beautiful book to the attention of the public.

I've been lucky enough to work with project editor Janet Illsley before, so I know just how much thought, insight and commitment she brings to a project. This one was no exception: she brought order to the chaos without losing its spontaneity, which is no mean feat. Recognition must also go to two other skilled and sensitive members of the editorial team – Sally Somers for her eagle-eyed proofreading and Hilary Bird for once again turning my non-linear thinking into an orderly index.

I'm grateful to various other people who gave advice or commented on versions of the constantly evolving typescript – these include the group of young, curious-minded people who offered their (sometimes scary) opinions on favourite foods: Nathaniel Cariss, Kirsty Farr, Vaila Henderson, Miles Trotter, Kathryn Leggett, Rico Gugolz, Luca Gugolz, Sam Winter, Millie Winter, Everley Hatton and Charlie Hatton. And also Annie Burns for her illuminating input on the mindful sandwich, Bronwen Jones and Rachel Calder for their editorial thoughts and good counsel, and Bhusana Premanode for his insights.

Book designer Dave Brown at Ape did that brilliant thing of taking my highly impressionistic briefing and turning it into exactly what I had in my head. He's another person who just totally 'got' this project and brought tons of commitment and imagination to it.

Photographers Liz Haarala and Max Hamilton likewise had to put up with my very scattergun approach to explaining myself and none the less created images that capture the beauty, intimacy and playfulness I was looking for. In this they were ably assisted by prop stylist Alexander Breeze and food stylist Valerie Berry, who were both from the get-go full of enthusiasm and brilliant ideas for how best to present the food.

Finally, what can I say about the genius that is Dave McKean? This is the third of my books he has illustrated. Each one has been transformed by his artwork but this time I think he's outdone himself – each image so full of sly, allusive, vivid, witty, energetic beauty. Every time I look at the pictures, I see something new.

To all of you – a *HUGE* thank you.

Internationally famous for his award-winning, 3-Michelin-starred restaurant, The Fat Duck, Heston Blumenthal is considered to be one of the best chefs of his generation.

Although self-taught, he has pushed the boundaries of the traditional kitchen and completely changed the way people approach cooking, introducing a new spirit of creativity, playfulness and experimentation, coupled with a deep sense of nostalgia and abiding interest in the history of British gastronomy. He has pioneered countless new techniques, from triple-cooked chips and fluid gels to food pairing and flavour encapsulation, in order to create a cuisine full of emotion and imagination. His food can be explored not just at The Fat Duck in Bray but also at Dinner by Heston Blumenthal, London, The Hind's Head in Bray, the Perfectionist's Café at Heathrow, Resonance bar and Dinner by Heston Blumenthal in Dubai.

He is the author of seven cookbooks, including *Heston at Home*, *The Big Fat Duck Cookbook* (winner of the Guild of Food Writers' Food Book of the Year), and *Historic Heston* (winner of the James Beard Foundation's Cookbook of the Year and the Guild of Food Writers' award for best work on British food).

Heston is an Honorary Fellow of The Royal Society of Chemistry and a Fellow of the Royal Academy of Culinary Arts. He has been awarded an honorary MSc by Bristol University, and honorary doctorates by Reading University and the University of London. In 2006 he was awarded an OBE by Her Majesty the Queen for his services to British gastronomy.

ABOUT THE ILLUSTRATOR

Widely acknowledged as one of the greatest illustrators at work today, Dave McKean's restless and inventive imagination finds expression in many forms and formats. He has illustrated countless books and graphic novels, including *The Wolves in the Walls* (winner of the New York Times Illustrated Book of the Year), *Varjak Paw* (winner of a Smarties Gold Award) and works by Stephen King, Ray Bradbury, William Gibson, Iain Sinclair and Richard Dawkins. He has worked with Neil Gaiman on several books, including *Coraline*, *Black Orchid*, *American Gods* and the iconic *Sandman* series. He also illustrated Grant Morrison's *Arkham Asylum*, which is the most successful graphic novel ever published.

Not content with this, he has also written theatre scripts, composed music, started a record label, created album covers for Michael Nyman, Tori Amos, The Misfits and Bill Bruford, among others, and made four films: *The Week Before*, *N[eon]* (which won First Prize at the Clermont-Ferrand Film Festival), *MirrorMask* (winner of nine awards, including the inaugural Black Tulip at the Amsterdam Fantastic Film Festival) and *Luma* (winner of Best British Feature and a BIFA at Raindance).

Since working with Heston on *The Big Fat Duck Cookbook*, Dave has illustrated *Historic Heston* and created many graphic works for The Fat Duck, the Hind's Head and Dinner by Heston Blumenthal, including package design, wallpaper, maps and murals. He is Director of Story at The Fat Duck.

A NOTE ON TYPE

Two principal typefaces are used in this book. For the 'Doing' pages: Sabon, a variant of Garamond created by Jan Tschichold in 1967 and prized for its elegance and legibility. For the 'Being' pages: Jacob Riley, created by Jessica McCarty in 2012, based on eighteenth-century printers' specimens, giving it a realistically expressive handwritten informality.

However, you might have noticed four divergences from this practice, where, with the assistance of graphic designer Sarah Hyndman, we have printed the title of a dish in a typeface (Cooper Black, Shatter, Ganache, Cheee) designed to complement that dish, perhaps even evoke its flavours or textures or emotional appeal.

As Heston has pointed out, our perception of flavour is highly subjective, influenced by mood, memories, expectations, associations and much else besides. So, can typography have an effect on taste? Well, when you make the tomato soup, fish & chips, mac 'n' cheese or panna cotta recipes in this book, why not take a look at the title as you eat it, and see what happens?

A NOTE ON HESTON'S COAT OF ARMS

On the first page of this book and below can be found Heston's coat of arms, for which he became eligible after being appointed OBE in 2006. A design was developed incorporating symbols of the five senses along with references to his life: outstretched hands for touch, discovery, empathy and shared connection; lyres for sound; an apple for taste and Newtonian investigation and inspiration; a magnifying glass for sight (and scientific exploration); lavender for smell and to recall the moment when he was inspired to become a chef in the lavender-scented gardens of the French restaurant L'Oustau de Baumanière. The duck refers to Heston's restaurant. Potentially landing or taking flight, it also symbolises change and evolution, while the three roses allude both to the heraldic Tudor rose of England and to the fact The Fat Duck has gained three Michelin stars. The motto below sums up Heston's approach to the world and cooking: Question Everything.

BLOOMSBURY PUBLISHING
Bloomsbury Publishing Plc
50 Bedford Square, London, WC1B 3DP, UK
29 Earlsfort Terrace, Dublin 2, Ireland

BLOOMSBURY, BLOOMSBURY PUBLISHING and the Diana logo are trademarks of
Bloomsbury Publishing Plc

First published in Great Britain, 2022

Text © Heston Blumenthal, 2022
Written in cooperation with Pascal Cariss
Illustrations © Dave McKean, 2022
Photographs © Haarala Hamilton, 2022
Cover photograph © Neale Haynes, 2022/Contour by Getty Images

A catalogue record for this book is available from the British Library

Library of Congress Cataloguing-in-Publication data has been applied for

ISBN: HB: 978-1-5266-2150-4; eBook: 978-1-5266-2152-8

2 4 6 8 10 9 7 5 3 1

Project Editor: Janet Illsley
Designer: Dave Brown, apeinc.co.uk
Illustrator: Dave McKean
Photographer: Haarala Hamilton
Food Stylist: Valerie Berry
Assistant Food Stylist: Hanna Miller
Prop Stylist: Alexander Breeze
Indexer: Hilary Bird

Printed and bound in Italy by Graphicom Spa

To find out more about our authors and books visit www.bloomsbury.com
and sign up for our newsletters